TEACHING ENGLISH in MISSIONS

Dr. Dormer has written an outstanding and much-needed text for Christians who are considering or are already involved in teaching English as a foreign/second language. She deals with several important issues that must be addressed today by English educators in both secular and Christian settings worldwide. Her focus on effectiveness and integrity is on target. Along with giving sound advice, practical tips, and concrete examples, she provides necessary cautions and asks key questions for careful consideration. Chapter 7 should be read and reread until it is internalized. As a longtime ESL educator, I wish I had read this book and had it in my professional library years ago. I highly recommend it.

J. Wesley Eby, author of *Handbook for Teaching Bible-Based ESL*
and many Bible studies for English learners

Exceptional! For any mission organization or for anyone using or hoping to use the teaching of English as a second or foreign language as a means of ministry opportunity, this book is a must-read. Jan Dormer has brought sense and sensitivity to a great ministry tool, protecting us from ministry abuse so common among those of us who rush in with zeal without knowledge. With a keen eye for any particular native culture and with a heart that cries "It's all about the student!" Jan dares to raise the level of expectation in missionary sensitivity, integrity, transparency, proficiency, authenticity, and competency. She makes me want to sign up! With an unequaled mix of the academic, missionary experience, and practical help, this book is bound to lead the way as the number-one textbook for this great endeavor.

Hubert Harriman, president, World Gospel Mission

If you're interested in English-language teaching and missions, this book is for you! Jan Dormer brings wide-ranging experience as a professional language educator and career missionary to her work and it shows. She tackles misconceptions, provides real-life illustrations, and offers practical, easy-to-understand guidelines in this reader-friendly introduction to English-language teaching and missions. While written primarily for those who are new to the area, this book can be read with benefit by anyone concerned with effectiveness and integrity in the ministry of English-language teaching.

Carolyn Kristjánsson, PhD
associate professor MA TESOL, Trinity Western University

As missions-minded agencies and individuals have sought to respond to the demand for English, the need for a book like *Teaching English in Missions* has increased. Jan Dormer's breadth of experience, lucid writing, and commitment to excellence in both teaching and ministry make this a must-read for every Christian involved in English-language teaching.

Kitty B. Purgason, PhD
associate professor, Department of Applied Linguistics and TESOL
Biola University
author of *English Language Teaching in Theological Contexts*

Jan Dormer's introduction to teaching English in mission is well grounded both in the English-teaching profession and the Christian faith. It makes an effective case for the importance of professionalism and integrity among missionaries who teach English, and also provides a great deal of useful guidance and practical information for missionary English teachers. Last and definitely not least, it does all of this in a very lucid and reader-friendly style.

Don Snow, PhD
author of *English Teaching as Christian Mission: An Applied Theology*
and *More Than a Native Speaker: An Introduction to Teaching English Abroad*

TEACHING ENGLISH *in MISSIONS*

EFFECTIVENESS *and* INTEGRITY

JAN EDWARDS DORMER

Published by William Carey Library
1605 E. Elizabeth Street
Pasadena, CA 91104 | www.missionbooks.org

Kelley K. Wolfe, editor
Rose Lee-Norman, copyeditor, indexer
Josie Leung, graphic designer
Cover photos © iStockphoto.com/evirgen

William Carey Library is a ministry of the
US Center for World Mission
Pasadena, CA | www.uscwm.org

17 16 15 14 13 5 4 3 2 1 SFP

Printed in the United States of America

Library of Congress Cataloging-in-Publication Data
Dormer, Jan Edwards.
Teaching English in missions: effectiveness and integrity/Jan Edwards Dormer.
p. cm.
Includes bibliographical references and index.
ISBN 978-0-87808-526-2
1. Missions--Educational work. 2. English language--Study and teaching--Foreign speakers. I. Title.
BV2630.D67 2011
266'.02—dc23

2011017807

To Rod
The stability behind my creativity

To Danna Jo and Jenna
Who grew up helping in English camps and classes,
and who never complained
about leading yet another group of English learners
in our unique rendition of "Lean on Me"

To my students all over the world
Who ultimately make it all worthwhile

CONTENTS

ACKNOWLEDGMENTS

I am deeply indebted to the Christian TESOL (Teaching English to Speakers of Other Languages) community for my continued formation as a Christian TESOL professional. Among this group of godly men and women are individuals who have encouraged my involvement in TESOL and cast a vision for me of what a Christian TESOL professional could look like. Articles, books, and conferences produced by this special community of believers have contributed much to my work overseas as a Christian English teacher and have helped shape my perspectives on what it means to engage in the teaching of English with effectiveness and integrity. In writing this book, several individuals took the time to read various chapters and provide me with invaluable feedback. I seek to pass on the mentorship I have received to those now entering the profession and Christian service.

INTRODUCTION

I think I started teaching English when I was twelve. I was a missionary kid (MK) in Brazil, and I remember Brazilian young people at our youth camps gathering around me to practice their English. Later in high school I actually earned a little money as an English tutor. But my real English-teaching career began in the United States several years later, as I taught for two years while acquiring an MA in TESOL in Indiana. I then married a Canadian pastor, moved to Ontario, and taught in both immigrant and international student programs for eight years.

The next bend in the road took us into missions, as we went with our two young daughters to Indonesia and worked with an international school for four years. There I taught both elementary and high school English learners. This was followed by a five-year stint in Brazil—"back home" for me. During this time I developed an English school, which grew to 150 students with programs for adults, teens, and children. While furloughing in Canada, we learned that the Brazilian government had unexpectedly denied our request for permanent visas. This led to our return to Indonesia. I was just completing a Doctorate of Education at the University of Toronto and spent the next four years developing a Master of Education program for Indonesian teachers while also teaching English in a seminary and a Muslim elementary school. Our next move took us back to the US for two years while preparing for our next assignment—a new ministry in Kenya.

I have taught English to all ages, at all language levels, in many different types of schools and programs, and to numerous ethnic and culture groups on four continents. To some, my diverse background may seem to have taught me nearly everything there is to know about teaching English in missions. How I wish this were true! Alas, I am painfully aware that there are many countries, teaching contexts, cultural issues, and government policies that I know absolutely nothing about. This reality nearly stopped me in my tracks and kept me from completing this book.

Then God spoke to me through what has been our lifelong ministry verse: "Each one should use whatever gift he has received, faithfully administering God's grace in its various forms" (1 Pet 4:10, NIV). This verse has given me confidence in numerous ministry situations in which I felt inadequate, from growing an English school in Brazil to teaching in a Muslim elementary school. With each difficult situation God has reassured me that I am only required to use the gifts that he has given me to bless others as I am able, and that I need be neither perfect nor infinitely wise. These qualities reside in God alone.

And so I introduce this book with the same perspective. I have used the gifts of education and experience that God has given me to provide the thoughts and suggestions on these pages. These are, I am certain, incomplete and imperfect. Nevertheless it is what I have to offer for those engaged in carrying out the Great Commission through English-language teaching.

THE TERM "MISSIONARY"

I like this word. I always have. Growing up as a missionary kid (MK) it had positive connotations for me of family (the mission family), hardships (the kind that make you feel good about the life you are living), and furloughs back home (where you get a year of really good food at church potluck dinners). I lament the negative and inaccurate connotation that it now has for some and the realities in certain contexts causing it to be replaced with less transparent terminology. I worked for eight years in a somewhat sensitive context and do understand that there are good reasons for not using the words "missions" and "missionary" in some places. Nevertheless, I have chosen to use these terms in this book.

My reasons for doing so are first because there does not seem to be another equivalent term. A "Christian English teacher" could be working in either his[1] own or a foreign country, paid or volunteer, sent by an agency or not. I have used this term when I talk about all Christian teachers. However, at times I wish to speak specifically of those who have left their home countries as Christian

1 In order to avoid cumbersome phrases such as "he or she" and "his or her," I alternate the use of gendered pronouns throughout this text.

cross-cultural workers supported by Christian sending organizations—and the most readily understood term for this type of person still seems to be "missionary." Second, I feel that my avoidance of this word will not increase security for those working in sensitive areas. Anyone who reads this book will be concerned with the ideas in these pages—not the words used to label those ideas.

EFL CONTEXT

This book is written with English as a Foreign Language (EFL) settings in mind. These are contexts in which English is not an official or commonly used language. I hope that much of the content in this book also holds value for those involved in English ministry in English-speaking countries—in English as a Second Language (ESL) settings. These ministries are just as important as those in traditional "mission field" settings. Individuals and churches engaged in the vital tasks of reaching immigrant groups and international students are having a tremendous impact, which I do not wish to diminish in any way. These teachers will, I hope, find value in these pages, even though ESL settings are not directly mentioned in this text.

INTENDED AUDIENCE

Prior experience or training in teaching English as a foreign language is not a requirement for reading this book. The acronym TESOL (Teaching English to Speakers of Other Languages) is used to talk about the field of English teaching. Apart from using this term, I have tried to keep the vocabulary simple and oriented to those outside the field of English-language teaching (however, a guide to TESOL acronyms is provided in Appendix F). I begin with perspectives that are held by many who are not trained English teachers and move on from there. I do hope that those who are more knowledgeable about the teaching of English will also find this book thought provoking. The particular way in which I relate the teaching of English to ministry may be new for some and will hopefully suggest some viable avenues for pursuing English teaching in missions. This book is for those interested in missions, whether trained English teachers or not, and an understanding of the Christian evangelical missionary enterprise is assumed.

OVERVIEW

The first two chapters are intended to expose common erroneous beliefs about English teaching in missions: first, that any native speaker can do it, and second, that English ministry is always beneficial. With this cautionary foundation set, I then proceed to construct a vision of what English ministry can look like. Chapter 3 highlights the purposes of evangelism and discipleship, within contexts that I label "ambassador" or "host." Chapter 4 focuses on the teacher, outlining the qualities and preparation necessary for teaching English as ministry. Chapters 5 and 6 bring theory to practice, focusing on the design and implementation of English programs and classes. Finally, Chapter 7 provides steps for bringing all this information together to make decisions about English ministry.

At the end of each chapter there are discussion and application activities. If this book is being used for teacher or ministry preparation, these questions and tasks may serve to help students reflect on and internalize what they have read.

EFFECTIVENESS AND INTEGRITY

Two unrelated events caused me to hone in on the words *effectiveness* and *integrity* in writing this book. The first was a conversation with a missionary colleague who asked me, "What do you mean when you say that English ministry should be *effective*?" That question struck me. At the time I felt that the answer was fairly self-evident, and I was surprised that my colleague would ask it. What else could it mean except that students should learn English and at the same time come closer to God? As I pondered this question, though, I realized that I did not have as precise a grasp as I thought I did on what constituted effectiveness. And so, I set out to discover what effectiveness might look like in English ministry. This book is my answer.

The other event was a momentary identity crisis as I sat in front of my computer registering for an English teachers' conference. The question that stumped me was "What affiliation would you like on your name badge?" I did not want to write the name of my mission organization, as I feared this would brand me as less professional than I was. However, I was also guilt ridden over my instinctive reaction to hide my affiliation. I finally settled on using the name of our local training institute, which was in a language that few could read anyway. It was either a cop-out or a clever compromise. But in either case, the professional/

missionary dichotomy was very real and troublesome. I felt I alternated between these two worlds, and longed for my worlds to blend rather than clash.

Over time I have come to see *integrity* as the only way forward in meshing these two worlds. *Encarta Dictionary* defines this word as "possession of firm principles" and "completeness, wholeness." If we wish to minister through English, we must first adhere to firm principles of quality and effectiveness in both English-language teaching and ministry. This provides us with a foundation for embracing wholeness—seeing ourselves as beings who are at the same time English teachers and ministers, just as one can be a doctor and a minister, or an accountant and a minister. We do not alternate these two hats; we wear them simultaneously. My English teaching is enhanced because I minister the love of Jesus Christ. My ministry is enhanced because I teach English. These two are not in competition, but rather are one complete identity in the person God created me to be. This is integrity.

My prayer is that these pages will highlight what *effectiveness* requires and what *integrity* demands. English ministry done with both has far-reaching potential.

CHAPTER 1

IF YOU CAN SPEAK ENGLISH YOU CAN TEACH IT. TRUE OR FALSE?

Bill[2] nervously entered the university classroom to find seventy eager students, facing him in neat rows. What in the world was he doing here, in an English class in Asia? He had majored in missions in college and had stayed as far away from the English department as possible. "If these students could see my high school English grades they would be leaving in droves," he thought wryly.

A few short weeks ago he had been so excited about this opportunity. His team leader had suggested that it would be a good way to meet people, and Bill could envision lively conversations and relationship building before and after class. He even thought he would invite some students to his house for coffee and get to know them better. But for some reason he hadn't given a whole lot of thought to this: the actual one hundred and twenty minutes during which time he was expected to stand at the front of the class and spew forth wisdom. In his planning and replanning for this moment he had come to one scary conclusion: he really had no idea what to do.

Bill's story is repeated frequently as more and more missionaries find themselves in English classrooms. It is difficult to find an evangelistically oriented mission organization that is *not* actively recruiting people to teach English. It is easy to see why: people all over the world want to learn English. Often they need English for work or studies. Sometimes they also want to understand English movies or songs or visiting tourists. And sometimes, they simply want the perceived status of being an English speaker. And so the mission community has seized this opportunity and built English teaching into its toolbox of techniques, often with self-proclaimed success. "Start an evangelical church in Poland, and no one will come. Start an English school, and you'll make many friends," says Agnieszka

2 Names of students and teachers in this text are pseudonyms; however, they represent real individuals or are composite sketches of individuals in real contexts.

Tennant (2002) in her *Christianity Today* article "The Ultimate Language Lesson." Another writer compares using English teaching with more tried and true missionary activities such as Bible studies and camps, saying, "Nothing appealed to the 'typical' German better than the English classes which we offered" (Woodward, 1993, p. 2).

And the desire is often reciprocal. Where missionaries want to teach English, locals are often desperate for a "native English speaker" to teach them. Even when missionaries do not want to teach English, they often face great local pressure to do so. What missionary has *not* heard the plea, "*Please* teach me English. I want to learn with a native English speaker."[3]

Of course not all missionaries who teach English are like Bill. Some are well trained as English teachers. But they seem to be in the minority. An informal survey in one mission organization revealed that on only two of twelve fields of service involved in English teaching was there someone who had training in teaching English as a foreign language. The prevailing message that is conveyed from both mission agencies who want people to send and locals who want to learn English is this: "If you can speak English, you can teach it." But, is this true?

To begin to answer this question, let's go back to Bill, to see how he's doing now, five minutes into the class.

As Bill finished taking attendance, struggling through the long list of unfamiliar names, he wished he had brought nametags for the students to wear. How could he call on anyone? Well, he would do this next time. Now for his first activity: introductions. "Hi. I'm Bill, and I'll be your teacher this semester. I'm from the US—North Dakota specifically. Does anybody know where that's at?" The silence was deafening. He had brought a small map, but only those in the first couple of rows could see it, so he quickly decided today was not going to be a day to learn about North Dakota.

Moving on . . . "Okay, I want you to turn to someone next to you and introduce yourself. Tell them your name and where you're from." The students sat silently, and it suddenly occurred to Bill that maybe they didn't know enough English to understand his instructions. So he pulled one surprised student out of her seat and acted out what he wanted them to do: "Hi, my name is Bill," he said loudly as he vigorously shook the hand of an obviously uncomfortable young woman.

3 Later we will see some possible negative effects when missionaries passively accept what has been called the "native speaker fallacy."

"What's yours?" he continued. The girl muttered something that he could not understand, but he decided to proceed. "Where are you from?" She said the name of the city that they were in, in a barely audible voice. As the young woman finally escaped to her seat, Bill motioned for all the students to do this in pairs. When they finally understood the task and turned to face each other, they did so with embarrassment. A few appeared to ask the questions very quietly, while others sat mutely in their seats doing nothing. The entire activity took about one minute. With perspiration forming on his forehead, Bill looked at his notes again, wondering how in the world he would last through 114 more minutes.

Bill is in trouble. And to understand the nature of his trouble, we need to first look at what is required for effective English teaching.

THE TWO REQUIREMENTS FOR LANGUAGE TEACHING

Effective language teachers possess two skill sets: 1) language skill and 2) teaching skill, as shown in Figure 1.

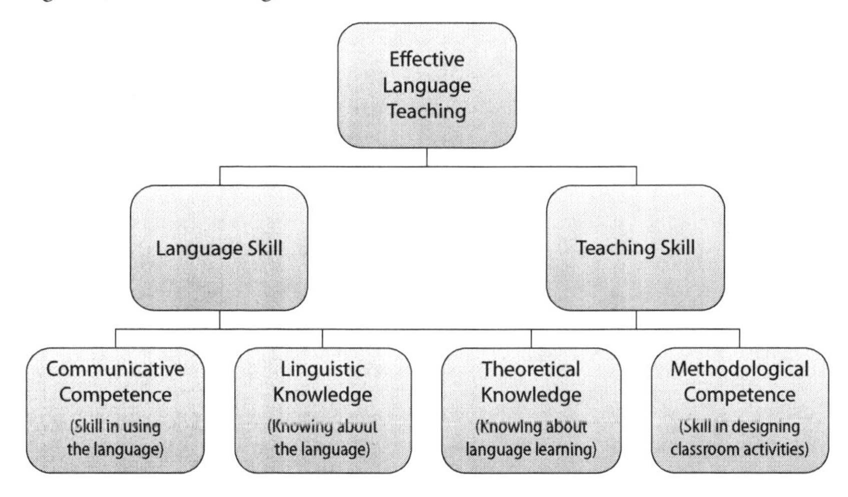

Figure 1. Requirements for effective language teaching

The first requirement seems obvious to most: You can't teach a language if you can't speak it. This ability to "speak" or "use" a language we call *communicative competence.* We develop this ability naturally in our native language. Usually by the age of five or six we are fully proficient in basic communication skills. We can both meet our needs and build relationships with others by using language.

Additionally, we are able to use language to think, entertain, and understand the world around us. But we do not automatically develop *linguistic knowledge*. This is knowing about language. Our teachers in school strive to fill our heads with an understanding of verbs and adjectives and adverbs, in hopes that we will know a lot about our language by the time we graduate from high school. Unfortunately, the result of many years of grammar study is often just a distaste for diagramming sentences—not a real and lasting understanding of how our language is put together.

Teaching skill is the second requirement for effective language teaching. In teacher education programs, the starting point for developing language teaching skill is *theoretical knowledge*. Language acquisition is a fascinating field of study. How does the brain make sense of incoming sounds and symbols and transform them into meaning? What conditions must be present for language acquisition, and why? When attempts at language learning fail, what has gone wrong?

After laying a foundation of theoretical understanding, we can begin to develop *methodological competence*—the ability to choose classroom activities and techniques which will result in language learning. We build up a storehouse of activities to teach the different language skills (speaking, listening, reading, and writing), different age groups, different class sizes, and multilevel classes (such as Bill's). We know how to foster *fluency* with some activities and *accuracy* with others. We can make quick changes in activities to perk up a sleepy class or to keep an overactive group of third-graders from tearing up the classroom. In essence, we know what to do in the classroom so that students can learn the language.

So now, let's check in on Bill again.

Bill has embarked on another of his planned activities: having students tell something they like to do. He began by saying "I like soccer," and writing the sentence on the board. Before he could even elicit student participation, an eager student in the third row shouted, "Teacher, I think 'to play soccer.'" Assuming that the student was his first eager participant, he enthusiastically affirmed the contribution, "Oh good! You like soccer too!" "No, no," came the reply, "You write 'I like soccer' but you must to write 'I like to play soccer.'" Bill was stumped. He had no idea how to explain why you could say it either way. And he had not planned on getting into any grammar—at least not today, and preferably never. He answered, "Well, it doesn't matter—you can say 'to play' or not—it doesn't matter." The student shook his head and gave a slight smile of superiority. Bill suspected that he had just lost at least one student's respect as an English teacher. How many more would follow? Would there be anything left to his teaching career after the next 105 minutes had passed?

Now Bill has gotten into a different kind of trouble: grammar trouble—what every untrained English teacher (and even some with training!) fears.

CAN BILL TEACH ENGLISH?

After seeing Bill's first fifteen minutes in the classroom, we have just about enough evidence to ascertain whether the statement "If you can speak English you can teach it" is true or false. Let's look at each of the competencies that are needed for effective language teaching and see how Bill fares.

Communicative competence

Bill *does* have communicative competence. He grew up in North Dakota and has spoken English all his life. He can use English very effectively in reading, writing, speaking, and listening. He gets 100% in this competency.

Linguistic knowledge

By his own admission, Bill "knows nothing about grammar." He made it through high school English by the skin of his teeth and wouldn't know a particle from an article. When he was studying the local language just recently, his teachers grew exasperated in trying to teach him clauses, because he didn't even understand them in English. I think we'll give him a 20% in this area for having a general idea of what verbs and nouns are, but even that is generous.

Theoretical knowledge

Some organizations provide new missionary candidates with a good understanding of language acquisition, but Bill's sending agency is not one of them. The extent of his preparation for language learning was receiving a list of tips such as "Get out with the people" and "Learn market language first." He learned nothing about concepts such as the silent period, interlanguage, fluency and accuracy, intrinsic and extrinsic motivation, the need to develop automaticity, learning styles, or fossilization. I think we'll give him 0% in this competency.

METHODOLOGICAL COMPETENCE

Does Bill know any good teaching methods? He probably does. After all, he has been in school for sixteen years. You can't sit in a classroom for that long without picking up some notion of how to teach. The question is, has Bill picked up any methods that are appropriate for *language* teaching? Learning a language is not like learning math, science, or even literature. If Bill studied a foreign language in high school or college, then *maybe* he has picked up some appropriate methods. However, language teaching in the United States has not produced stellar results in the past, as evidenced by the overabundance of Americans who are monolingual. So there's a good chance that Bill does not have a great many language-teaching methodologies tucked away from his high school and college French classes.

What about his recent experiences in learning the local language? This may possibly help him, but sadly, some language school programs for missionaries do not have teachers who are well trained in language-teaching methodology. Some use methodologies with limited effectiveness, forcing missionaries to acquire much of the language from their own initiative. Even if Bill has experienced good methodology in his local language classes, these were probably for a very small group of people, and he has still probably not seen methodologies which could be used in a class of seventy. So, again, Bill's chances for having passively acquired appropriate methods as a language student are slim.

What about natural ability? Bill probably has some knack for teaching. He shows potential here, despite his rather dismal first fifteen minutes. He got students working in pairs. He introduced a topic of interest (hobbies). He made a statement orally and also wrote it on the board: good reinforcement and simultaneous development of oral and written skills. I could work with this guy! I'll give him a 30% just for raw ability and intuition.

THE VERDICT

Bill's score is 150 out of 400 total points. That's 37%. Not the greatest. So, should Bill pack up his briefcase and be done with English teaching? Not necessarily. First, preparatory programs for teaching English abound, even online, and in a short time of study Bill could significantly increase his score in language-teaching effectiveness. Second, we will see later in this book the vast diversity of English-teaching contexts and the fittedness of individuals with differing competencies for different types of teaching. For example, there are students who simply need conversation partners, and Bill could do that well. Third, there are contexts in which untrained teachers are supervised and helped by trained teachers. Bill could also work well in this kind of environment. So, he should not despair just yet.

However, it behooves us to look at Bill's case and his lack of skills in three of the four major areas and admit what his first fifteen minutes have made painfully clear to him: Bill is not an English teacher. Both uninformed missionaries and their sending agencies and uninformed local people clamoring for a native English speaker are wrong: simply being able to speak a language does *not* mean you are able to teach it.

This fact is supported and affirmed by every major professional organization for language teaching. TESOL (Teachers of English to Speakers of Other Languages) is the largest worldwide professional organization for English-language teachers. A position statement posted on their website states:

> English language learners, whether in an English as a second language (ESL) or English as a foreign language (EFL) setting, have the right to be taught by qualified and trained teachers. Native speaker proficiency in the target language alone is not a sufficient qualification for such teaching positions; the field of teaching English to speakers of other languages (TESOL) is a professional discipline that requires specialized training. (TESOL, 2003)

Failure to recognize this fact is akin to sending people out to teach theology on the basis of their knowledge of Bible stories. No mission agency that I know of would do this. The rationale for lower standards for English teaching is sometimes the belief that even if English teachers don't know what they're doing, they can't really cause any harm. "Anything is better than nothing," is the perception. But is it? This is the topic of our next chapter.

DISCUSSION AND APPLICATION

1. Have you or has someone you know been in a situation similar to Bill's? Describe the situation and the outcome.
2. Give yourself a grade in each of the skill areas for effective teaching. How do you measure up? If you plan on becoming an English teacher, what areas do you most need to develop?
3. Has this chapter convinced you that simply speaking a language is not sufficient qualification for teaching it? If not, what are your reservations?

CHAPTER 2

"FIRST, DO NO HARM": AN ENGLISH TEACHER'S HIPPOCRATIC OATH

The injunction in this title to "do no harm" usually relates to the practice of medicine. As a profession, the medical community declares that, first and foremost, medical practices must not cause a person harm. In English teaching, likewise, we seek to never inadvertently cause harm as we strive to meet real and felt language needs.

When told that English teaching in missions can, if not done well, result in harm, those in ministry frequently react with disbelief. After all, the call to missions is largely a call to serve and help others. Missionaries and sending organizations do all they do for the sole purpose of bettering the lives of others and never intend to do harm.

VALUING THE PAST

And so, before getting into the potential "harms," I want to first acknowledge the great good that has often occurred through English ministries. On a spiritual level, English teaching has often provided an excellent context within which to build relationships with people and engage in spiritual dialogue. As Christian English teachers have lived out their faith in the classroom, those who did not know Christ have had firsthand opportunities to see the love, joy, and peace that he brings. They have been in an environment in which questions and personal sharing are appropriate, and thus have been able to investigate the Christian faith. Many English learners in such environments have chosen to follow Christ as a result. In our worldview, this is the greatest good that could happen to a person.

On an English-learning level, students have benefited as well, even when teachers have been untrained. It would indeed be rare for nothing at all to be learned in an English class, regardless of the level of preparation the teacher has for English teaching. And often, student learning has not been minimal but substantial. There have been English-teaching pioneers in missions who, though lacking credentials, have engaged in exceptional work. Some have produced materials that continue to bless English-teaching ministries today and others have become self-taught, excellent English teachers.

The goal of this chapter is not to in any way diminish these benefits. We have arrived at the insight that we possess today only by building on the work of those who came before us. There are countless individuals across the globe who would stand up today and say, "My English teacher was great. I learned a lot of English, but even more importantly, I came to know the Lord. I wouldn't trade my experience for anything." These learners' voices are important.

HEARING OTHER VOICES

But these are not the only voices we should listen to as we seek to measure our past effectiveness in using English teaching in missions and to design effective English-ministry programs for the twenty-first century. We must also listen to the voices of our critics. Are there any students who perhaps have *not* achieved their English goals in our classes? Do students ever feel pressured or coerced into spiritual discussions or decisions? Are there local English teachers who feel that their jobs and respect are unfairly usurped by untrained foreign missionary teachers? Are all societies benefitted by the ever-greater push to learn English? Many in the field of English teaching have been looking at these and other questions. We will endeavor in this chapter to "hear" these other voices.

A NEW WORLD IN ENGLISH EDUCATION

The field of English teaching in *English as a Foreign Language (EFL)* settings, places where English is not the main language of communication, is different today than it was twenty-five years ago. English used to be a specific skill needed by some students, business people, and perhaps a few in other professions. People learned it for instrumental reasons, to further their academic or professional careers. It was also often a foreign language subject in school, but as such it was most often considered academic knowledge rather than a needed skill. In addition, English teaching and learning invariably had a connection to English-speaking countries or native English speakers. Students prepared to study abroad in an English-speaking country or prepared to interact with foreigners from those countries through business or tourism. When taught as an academic subject, English was taught as belonging to people in English-speaking countries.

The landscape of English learning is quite different today. No one can deny the fact that in our shrinking, twenty-first-century world, English has emerged as the lingua franca. This has brought with it several new realities. First, English is no longer seen as the possession of the traditional English-speaking countries. There are already more people who speak English as an additional language than those who speak it as a native language. And even the term "native speaker" has begun to embody different realities as more and more countries adopt English as an additional national language or as a language of instruction in schools. Kachru, in 1985, coined the term "world Englishes," and demonstrated global English usage in concentric circles (Figure 2). He called the traditional English-speaking countries the *center* or *inner circle.* Countries which have more recently emerged as English dominant, such as India and Singapore, he labeled the *outer circle.* Beyond this is the *expanding circle,* sometimes called the *periphery.* Here we find countries in which English is becoming more and more important, though still a *foreign* language. Kachru's concept of world Englishes can help us to understand that we are now moving beyond North American English or British English to include varieties such as Indian English, Singaporean English, and African English.

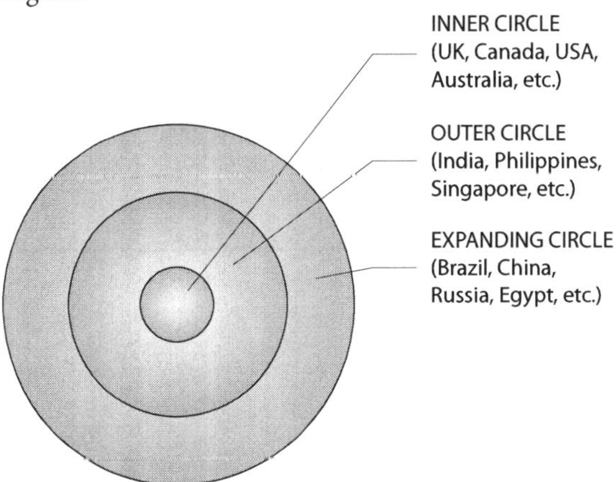

Figure 2. World Englishes (adapted from Kachru, 1985)

In addition, there is a growing movement among teachers in favor of teaching English as an International Language (EIL), especially in periphery countries. However, an adequate description of what International English is has not yet emerged. In the past, descriptions of languages largely hinged on how the native speakers of those languages used them. But if we envision a language such as International English, will it have native speakers? Will there be the kind of culture-language connections that currently figure prominently in language teaching? Researchers are divided on these questions. But even as researchers debate, one thing is clear: many teachers around the globe like the *idea* of International English, and we will likely see this movement develop and take hold in the coming years. It is possible that the content of a typical English curriculum in the future will look quite different from those of today. For example, the holidays and customs of English-speaking countries—currently typical fare in English course books—may no longer be relevant for a student learning English in Thailand in order to communicate with a Japanese businessman.

A final and significant driving force in English learning today comes not from researchers and teachers, but from the consumers of English courses in EFL contexts. For many, English is no longer seen as optional, but as a required life skill. Parents all over the world place ever-younger children in English classes, believing that a good future is not possible for them without English. University students and adults enroll in English classes for fear of not getting into educational programs or not getting job promotions. Such beliefs and global realities have resulted in a huge world market for English and educational institutions that are often driven more by consumer demand than by language-learning principles.

I will provide here two examples of educational trends that are fueled by market demand rather than language-acquisition research. 1) Untrained native English speakers are hired as English teachers instead of trained non-native English-speaking teachers. 2) Classes are being offered for ever-younger students—sometime as young as age two. In each of these examples, research stands in opposition to public opinion. Native speakers are *not* better language teachers simply by virtue of being native speakers. And, "the younger the better" is *not* a given in language learning. We will look at each of these myths later in relation to specific harms that they can cause. But the point here is that these decisions are made to gain clients—clients who may hold false assumptions about language learning. And this brings to light an additional problem:

leaders and teachers in educational institutions often have little background in language acquisition and cannot themselves distinguish myth from reality. Such is the English-teaching and English-learning world in many EFL contexts today, in which demand has so far outstripped the supply of knowledgeable personnel that virtually anyone can start an English school and make a profit by catering to the uninformed opinions of the population at large.

As these new realities permeate the field of English teaching and learning, we need to stop and consider their possible ramifications. Yes, the spread of English and its consumer-driven orientation can be viewed as "open doors" for ministry. Native English speakers need do little more than "show up" in some parts of the world to have an eager audience for whatever ideas they hold dear—such is the intense desire to practice English with a native speaker. But we need to see beyond such opportunities to dangers that may lurk behind them. Snow (2009) says, "While Christian missionaries generally have not intended to advance the world role of English per se, they have certainly been an important part of the process, and I believe this legacy calls Western Christian English teachers to consider what obligations it leaves them with" (p. 175).

I believe that we can minister to others through the forum of English teaching, as the rest of this book will affirm. However, we cannot do so effectively without first taking an honest look at how we could also inadvertently bring harm. In a world where English competence is sometimes seen as being as important as literacy itself, the spread of English may cause societal, cultural, educational, and even spiritual harm if we do not proceed cautiously, sensitively, and prayerfully.

POTENTIAL HARMS IN ENGLISH LANGUAGE TEACHING

SOCIETAL HARM

In 1992 Phillipson wrote a book entitled *Linguistic Imperialism,* which outlines injustices and inequalities perpetrated through the spread of English. Many feel that Phillipson's allusion to a cultural elite in English-speaking countries that is actively trying to promote the spread of English is somewhat overstated. However, the fact that English is spreading so rapidly, whether due to anyone's evil intent or not, does mean that we need to step back and look at the possible outcomes of this phenomenon.

Phillipson (1992) asserts that the English-learning tidal wave sweeping the world does not promote equality for all, but rather exacerbates already existing inequalities. He states, "One characteristic of the majority of Third World countries in which English is a dominant language is that the wealth that English provides access to is very inequitably distributed" (p. 11). De Mejia (2002), in *Power, Prestige and Bilingualism: International Perspectives on Elite Bilingual Education* agrees, saying that as those who can afford education rush to acquire English, inevitably the divide between the "haves" and the "have nots" is increased. Whatever our perspectives on economics and societal inequalities, we need to be aware that as English learning provides advantages for those who have access to it, it simultaneously makes life more difficult for those who don't.

Another societal harm comes through the ever-increasing demand for native speakers, a point touched on earlier. Unfortunately, the preference for native English-speaking teachers sometimes results in local, nonnative English-speaking teachers losing or not being able to get jobs. As we have already seen from Bill's story in Chapter 1, the ability to speak English is only one of several skills that are necessary for effective teaching. But the general population is unaware of this, and they urge schools to hire native English speakers regardless of the cost—and often native English speakers cost much more. Untrained native English speakers may earn three or four times the salary of a local, trained, nonnative English speaker. (See Braine, 1999, on the inequalities faced by nonnative-speaking teachers of English.) Many such local teachers are quite proficient in the English language and have excellent teaching skills. By all rights they should be earning more than their untrained, native English-speaking counterparts, but they do not.

In missions we may feel absolved from causing teachers to lose jobs if we do not charge for our services. But this brings suspicion and ill will of a different sort. In an article entitled "Responding to Job Competition from Native Speakers," Marcia Fisk Ong states that "some evangelists offer language lessons at no cost with the hope of gaining converts. They sometimes even disguise their actual missions. Some enter the field of English teaching with a certificate from a training course as short as three days" (Abelaira, et al., 2004). The fact that we may not charge is seen not as helpful, but as deceptive. And we may *still* be viewed as taking jobs away from local teachers.

Cultural harm

Schiller (1976) used the label "cultural imperialism" to describe a society which is being brought into the modern world and pressured or lured into adopting new values and systems. Though English classes may not bear nearly as much responsibility for the emerging global culture as movies, music, and the internet, they nevertheless play a role. When teaching Muslim students I have at times skipped many units in a required text because the images or values in them were at odds with the values held by my students. Sometimes they were at odds with my own values as well. Unfortunately, many teachers never consider that any portion of the book might be inappropriate; such is their lack of reflection concerning the promotion of values in the English classroom. And thus the cultural values of textbook creators are blindly embraced.

Such cultural ignorance is also seen in methodology. Bahloul (1994), in an article entitled "The Need for a Cross-cultural approach to Teaching EFL," outlines a scenario in which native English-speaking teachers come into a school setting that values traditional grammar instruction and attempt to quickly replace such instruction with communicative teaching methods. Such teachers are painfully unaware of the possible ramifications of such changes: students may not pass national tests because they lack solid grammar training, local teachers who continue to teach in traditional ways may lose respect because they are being compared to the exciting native English-speaking teacher, and parents may complain because the tangible evidence of English learning—completed grammar books—is missing. I have certainly done my share of promoting change in curriculum, texts, and methodology in English programs. However, such changes should happen in partnership with local English teachers and should never be initiated without considering the consequences.

As the English language and related culture encroaches, local languages and cultures may diminish in perceived importance. McKay (2002) states two negative effects of the spread of English: "the threat to existing languages" and "the influence on cultural identity" (p. 20). Indonesia is a case in point. Twenty years ago, most children spoke ethnic languages at home (e.g., Javanese, Sundanese, Balinese) and learned the national language of *Bahasa Indonesia* ("Indonesian" in English) in school. Perhaps they had foreign language instruction in English, for one or two periods a week. But today many children speak Indonesian at home, not an ethnic language. These same children, if their parents can afford it, will attend private schools which teach 50–95 percent of the subject matter in English. The bilingual school trend is gaining such popularity that some public schools are also attempting to become "bilingual." There is a grave threat to academic achievement in such schools, as we will soon discuss. But the point in terms of culture is that in such schools even the national language takes a backseat to English. Many of these schools are attempting to become "fully English"—relegating both Indonesian and heritage languages to a few hours of instruction per week. The national language can survive on some level, as the majority use it for daily communication. But ethnic languages will not fare well in such an environment.

Language change is inevitable, and language loss is sometimes unavoidable. The danger, I believe, lies in blindly promoting the learning of English without anticipating the possible impact on local language and culture. We in missions have, perhaps more than many groups, supported, encouraged, and helped to maintain minority and ethnic languages. Wycliffe Bible Translators has done a tremendous job in this regard. Though those outside the Christian community do not appreciate their ultimate goals of evangelism, no one denies their expertise in linguistics or their contributions to the maintenance of minority languages. We need to continue on in this tradition, voicing a concern over the neglect and demise of languages and cultures. Typically when I give seminars on bilingual education in Indonesia and voice my professional opinion that heritage languages in Indonesia will be virtually absent from common usage in many places in another generation, many teachers are stunned. They often have not considered that using English as the language of instruction in their schools could have this effect. Though I cannot stop the loss of languages in Indonesia, I *can* help teachers and schools to consider these possibilities and possibly make more informed choices regarding languages of instruction.

EDUCATIONAL HARM

The ways in which the advance of English may cause harm educationally are numerous. First, it may actually result in poor English learning. *Fast* educational development often means *poor* educational development, and the teaching of English is no exception. The demand for English has far outpaced many countries' capabilities for producing good English teachers and good materials. This means poorly prepared teachers in classrooms, ineffective class sessions, and thousands of dollars wasted on unproductive classroom time. Even private schools, which frequently pay higher salaries, often struggle to find appropriately trained personnel. And in some cases, there is not a clear understanding of what "appropriately trained" means. When English proficiency is considered the only requirement for teaching English, as it is in many places, teachers (including native English speakers) may have little understanding about what needs to take place in the classroom to promote language learning.

Second, as we have already seen, the focus on English may result in a lack of attention to the native or national language. Though research overwhelmingly shows us that it is beneficial for a child to develop a high level of his or her first language (Cummins, 2000), many teachers and school leaders are unaware of this. As more and more English is crammed into the school day and after-school activities, less time is available for developing students' competence in their native language. When the lack of focus on the native language is coupled with poor English instruction, *semilingualism* can result—the lack of attainment of proficiency in *any* language to an academic level sufficient for success in higher education (Cummins, 1994). This is indeed a travesty.

A third harm may be seen in bilingual and full-English immersion schools. According to De Mejia (2002), many bilingual schools in EFL settings show poor results in both language and academic development. When English is the language of instruction for academic content, but both teachers and students are ill prepared for classes conducted in English, academic deficiencies can result. When teachers lack sufficient English to explain science concepts, for example, and students lack sufficient English to understand the concepts, English learning is not the only thing that suffers: science learning suffers as well.

Finally, a result of the increased focus on English is that children are being forced into English classes at ever-younger ages, as was mentioned earlier, and poor early childhood development may result. Parents who place their children in English classes at two or three years of age believe they are giving them an advantage in life. But there is no evidence that such early learning is either necessary or helpful. According to Phillipson (1999), "Few if any scholars in bilingual education or foreign language pedagogy would endorse without qualification the belief that 'the earlier the better' is the key solution to second or foreign language learning, since there is massive scientific evidence to the contrary" (p. 56). If an English class at age two is not necessary, still, is it *harmful?* I suggest that it can be. When children begin formal instruction too early they are not allowed the natural cognitive, emotional, and linguistic development that occurs through play and interaction with caregivers. Such children are not learning two languages simultaneously and naturally, as is the case when each of the parents speaks a different native language, or a caregiver speaks a language different from the parents. Rather, these children are in formal school settings, sometimes learning English from teachers who are barely proficient in English themselves. They are also not allowed adequate time to focus on developing their native language—a crucial task in the preschool years.

SPIRITUAL HARM

As unfortunate as it may be for English to adversely affect society, culture, or education, a much more serious threat is the potential spiritual harm that can result if English teaching in ministry is misguided or ill conceived. When helping people achieve spiritual well-being is our goal, it can be hard to even consider the possibility that we could actually drive people away. I will highlight here three ways in which Christian English teachers could inadvertently cause spiritual harm.

First, I believe that spiritual harm can result if the English-teaching ministry involves any kind of *deception*. This is one of the strongest accusations leveled at the missionary English-teaching enterprise, as exemplified in this statement by Edge (2003): "If, for some people, religious conversion is their goal and TESOL is their means, then I believe that these people have a moral duty to make that instrumental goal and means relationship absolutely explicit at all stages of their work" (p. 704).

There are many biblical commands involving truthfulness. We are to be honest and forthright in our dealings with others. Why should anyone want to learn anything from us if we are not? If we are presenting ourselves as English teachers, then we must *be* English teachers. Amazingly, there are those who seek degrees in English or TESOL for visa purposes alone. They do not even plan on teaching. I spoke with one young woman at a Christian college who unabashedly told me, "I'm majoring in English education because, you know, it's easy to get a visa to get into country X that way. I'm not going to teach English. I'm just going to work with the people." One has to wonder at this distorted view of education and vocation. Thousands of dollars are being wasted on an education that is not expected to be used. Studies that might actually help her "work with the people" are not being sought. And, she is actively planning to enter a country under false pretenses.

Others do actually use their teaching degrees or certificates to teach English, but do so solely for the purpose of building relationships with local people and do not fully engage in their jobs as English teachers. This, too, is deceptive. Wong (2009) states:

> Viewing teaching as only a "creative access" is treating it as just a means to an end. This distorted view of "tentmaking" is inappropriate because those who use teaching and do not *engage* in it devalue the profession, their students, and their primary calling as Christ followers. (p. 93)

Unfortunately missionary "covert ops" seem attractive to some Western supporters, who appear to think that the more code in the prayer letter or the more secretive the work, the more spiritual the ministry. We who work in "closed" countries must actively seek to increase transparency to the degree possible in any given context, in both the country of ministry and in sending countries.[4] We need to make an effort to educate supporters about real rather than over-sensationalized political and religious realities in the countries in which we serve. We should emphasize respect for governments and their laws, honesty and integrity in gaining entrance into countries, and transparency in who we are. Many Christian English-teaching professionals work openly in countries that are closed to missionaries. Research done by Loptes (2009) on Christian English teachers working in countries restricting missionary activity highlights the fact that English-teaching professionals can be salt and light by doing their jobs well and abiding by local laws with regard to sharing their faith. Romanowski and McCarthy (2009) affirm this:

> Christian educators are called to be just that—Christian teachers, instructors or professors who strive to impact their students' lives with truth, integrity and honesty. Undercover Christian teachers may have some impact, but it is limited and their impact is in spite of their motives, not as a result of them. (p. 16)

4 The issue of transparency in missions is a controversial and complex one. Political and religious contexts which may not welcome missionary activity are diverse and unique, and I do not intend to suggest here that there is a universally appropriate approach to this issue. However, I do suggest that missionary activity has sometimes suffered from a lack of transparency, and we need to move toward transparency whenever, however, and wherever possible.

I am well aware that missionaries often wear many hats, and the "English-teaching hat" may be a minor one in the overall ministry picture. Other chapters in this book will, I believe, address issues of professional preparation and integrity on many different levels of involvement in TESOL in missions. The point made here is that those who enter a country with an English-teaching visa must actually engage in the teaching of English and make teaching English well a top priority. The corollary to this point is that those unwilling to view English teaching in this way should *not* seek English-teaching visas. In some sending organizations such a shift of perspective could lead to sending out fewer but better-prepared English teachers. This, in my view, would be a change for the better.

A second spiritual harm may come from *misrepresenting the gospel.* This may happen when Christian English teachers confuse what is cultural and political with what is Christian. In some churches in the US it is not unusual to hear statements to the effect that "God has blessed America, and it is the greatest nation on earth." Those who have grown up hearing such statements may not have a properly developed understanding that God is working around the globe, in all different cultures and amidst many different political systems. Smith (2009) narrates the perspective of a person with this limited understanding:

> I have little expectation that God is saying things to members of the other culture that I need to hear, or that *they* will teach *me* obedience or challenge *my* sin. God speaks my language and likes my ways, and must surely share my discomfort at the strange ways of others. (p. 21)

Johnston (2009), a critic of missionary English teaching, believes that "it is undeniable that the practice of much evangelical Christianity is bound up with politics and business at least as much as it is with religious beliefs" (p. 40). We can hope that it is not so and that those who go overseas to minister can separate Christianity from politics and culture. But the fact is that English teachers are often the least prepared theologically, and sometimes culturally, for overseas ministry. English teaching tends to fall under short-term missions and as such sometimes requires little ministry preparation. If a short-term candidate has strong notions linking democracy and capitalism to Christianity, for instance, it is unlikely that the minimal preparation often required for short-term service will lead to reflection on these deeply held beliefs or raise awareness of the potential harm in espousing such beliefs alongside the Christian faith, especially in countries with different political and economic systems.

Short-term missionaries who have a limited, culturally defined view of God and the gospel are also often individuals who feel compelled to convince others about the rightness of their beliefs. They may view ministry as convincing and converting rather than as meeting the needs of students. Pennycook and Coutand-Marin (2003), in an accusing article entitled "Teaching English as a Missionary Language" assert:

> The moral project of EML [English as a Missionary Language] all too often lacks an adequate ethics. While religious thinking is supposed to encourage an engagement with hard ethical questions, all too often it does little more than promote a prior moral absolutism. By this we mean that this approach to thought and education operates with an overarching moral position that does not allow for ethical response. (p. 351)

In contrast, Byler (2009) states, "A truly Christ-like presence among language students will not focus on targeting and strategizing for conversion, but rather be concerned with the needs of the students" (p. 128).

So what does it mean to represent the gospel well through English teaching? It means first that we must conscientiously critique the cultural baggage that may be present in our understanding of the gospel and be willing to lay that baggage aside as we contemplate how God is working in, among, and through those we have come to serve. And second, it means seeing ourselves as servants of our students, modeling our actions after the servanthood of Christ rather than as on a mission to convince our students of the rightness of our beliefs.

This leads us to the final type of spiritual harm: *coercion.* Most Christian evangelical missionaries would be adamantly opposed to any kind of coercion tactics in order to gain converts. In fact, the Bible emphasizes that a person should come to Christ of his or her own free will (Acts 2:37–41). What some in cross-cultural ministry are not aware of, however, is that the combination of positions of authority ("teacher") and cultural norms may result in unintended coercive situations. Chamberlain (2009) recounts one such experience:

> While I was on a mission stint in my college years, one of my "students" and I became "friends." Months later, he disclosed

> through a letter that he had "faked conversion" so that he could spend time with me. In his mind, "free" classes came at a cost—conversion. (p. 49)

Edge (2003) has painted an even more dire picture of the issues of power and coercion in English teaching:

> Perhaps one way to understand the threat involved is to reverse the relationships. We need to imagine ourselves as constrained to encourage members of our community, perhaps send out our children (for as anyone involved in worldwide TEFL [Teaching English as a Foreign Language] knows, both in the public and private sectors, the major growth area is in the teaching of English to ever-younger learners) to learn a language essential for their educational development and material well-being. We are required to do this in the knowledge that an unknown number of the teachers of that language are there with the express purpose of subverting our most deeply held beliefs and taking those people, those children, from us. (p. 705)

As a Christian missionary, this is a wake-up call for me to think of how I would feel were the teachers of my children trying to turn them away from my deeply held beliefs.[5] It is also sobering to recall that in times past children in some places *were* taken from their parents by Christians in an effort to evangelize and assimilate them. We must face and acknowledge such misguided actions, rather than being defiant in the face of criticism. Careful soul-searching and reflection, coupled with an honest look at whether or not our English-teaching ministries may hint of coercion, is the only appropriate response.

We cannot change the fact that a teacher holds a position of power and that there are cultural contexts in which it may be difficult to communicate the Western notion that students do not need to believe what the teacher believes, and in fact are encouraged to form their own beliefs. But simply being aware of these issues can help to lessen the likelihood that Chamberlain's story above will be repeated.

5 Chapter 4 addresses some of the ethical issues that are important in ministry with children.

CONCLUSION

Christians believe that the Bible is the revealed truth about God, and that it is for all people, everywhere. We certainly must hold tightly to this belief, for without it there is no gospel. And the opportunities for Christians to teach English in all parts of the globe are tremendous. But we must tread very carefully as we represent Christ in and through English classes. Pennycook and Coutand-Marin (2003) have said, "Once ELT [English Language Teaching] becomes constructed in itself as a form of Christian service, it is also too easy for the promotion of ELT to be driven by missionary fervor rather than educational need" (p. 348). Has this happened? Do we sometimes now teach English in missions simply because it has become a form of missionary service, without seeing its possible negative consequences? Or are we actively looking at our ministries and ensuring that they are not harmful but helpful in every possible way? The remainder of this book aims to provide tools to help us do this.

DISCUSSION AND APPLICATION

1. How do you think the concept of *world Englishes* might impact the teaching of English in missions?
2. What is your understanding of *linguistic imperialism*? Suggest an approach to English ministry, in a specific context, that could minimize the effects of linguistic imperialism.
3. Choose one of the four harms outlined in this chapter. Imagine that you are providing training for short-term missionaries going out to teach English for a semester. What information or guidelines would you provide to help them avoid this harm?
4. Choose a mission context that you are familiar with. Address each of the four harms in relation to this context, demonstrating how English teaching can avoid causing harm in this context.

CHAPTER 3

ENGLISH MINISTRIES WITH INTEGRITY: FOUR TYPES

The dangers we have seen in Chapter 2 should serve to caution us, not cause us to abandon English ministries altogether. Though we should be ever vigilant to reduce or eliminate the potential harms whenever and wherever we can, the fact is that English teaching will go on with or without us. Having teachers who approach English teaching cautiously, humbly, and knowledgeably, and not arrogantly, benefits students. If we are willing to serve our students from such a posture, we can pursue English ministries that will maximize benefit and minimize risk. So, we now turn our attention in a more positive direction for the remainder of the book, looking at the exciting ways in which the teaching of English can be a part of God's purposes and plans. In this chapter we look at various types of English ministries and what effectiveness may look like within these different contexts.

WHAT ENGLISH MINISTRY IS NOT

At the outset, though, it is important to make clear what English ministry with integrity is not. There is strong consensus among Christian professionals in the field of TESOL that there is no place in Christian ministry for English teaching whose only goal is evangelism (see Wong and Canagarajah, 2009). If we do not also care that our students learn English, we have no business being in an English classroom. If English teaching is only a way to get a visa, this is a misrepresentation of identity and intent and thus is not an endeavor of integrity. So as we discuss the purposes and perspectives of English ministries in this chapter, the given premise is that there is genuine desire to teach English to the best of one's ability and to meet learners' English needs. Chapters 5 and 6 deal more specifically with effectiveness in teaching English.

English ministry is also not placing the English language, and its teachers, in a position of superiority over the host language and culture. Missionaries have often led the way in valuing local cultures and languages and fighting for their value even when colonizing forces have not (see Makoni and Makoni, 2009, in reference to indigenous languages in Africa, for example). This is the heritage we should emulate. Being involved in English ministries should never be an excuse for not learning the local language and culture. Snow (2009) has argued that,

> as speakers of a powerful language who are concerned with issues of dominance and power, one response should be at times to step out of the power role by becoming learners of other languages, both because of how the experience of learning the other's language transforms us and because of the message that such a choice sends about our vision of what kind of place we think the world should be. (p. 183)

In this chapter we will not be talking about English goals and teacher-learning goals, which must be part and parcel of any English-teaching situation. In later chapters we will deal more with teacher preparation. Here, we will discuss the *ministry* goals that are unique to the English-ministry enterprise.

PURPOSES OF ENGLISH MINISTRIES

I propose two ministry-related purposes for teaching English in missions: evangelism and discipleship. I use *evangelism* in its broadest sense here, encompassing a continuum of ideas and activities. At one end of the spectrum we would find simply a desire to fulfill Christ's command to be salt and light wherever we go, with an ultimate hope that others may have opportunities to know him. I include in this category efforts such as peacemaking and educational development, endeavors in which we as Christians must be engaged. However, my perspective is that we embody the gospel in these efforts, working for the redemption of relationships and societies through the power of Jesus Christ.[6] At the other end of the evangelism spectrum, we may find overt activities such as Bible studies and the showing of evangelistic films.

---

6 Some may feel that the term "evangelism" is inappropriate for activities which do not actively involve "sharing the gospel." Some may prefer the term "pre-evangelism" and others may feel that efforts to simply be the salt and light of Christ amidst those who do not know Him are not best framed as "evangelism." See Don Snow's book *English Teaching as Christian Mission: An Applied Theology* (2001) for a broader framework for these types of English ministries.

Discipleship, on the other hand, involves working with those who are already believers, helping them grow in their faith. This may be in Christian settings such as seminaries or Christian schools, or in other less-formal activities such as tutoring combined with Christian mentorship.

PERSPECTIVES OF ENGLISH MINISTRIES

We also find two possible perspectives from which English ministries are conducted: that of *ambassador* or that of *host.* The ambassador perspective is that of an invited guest, whose purpose it is to build bridges and promote goodwill. A good ambassador maintains his identity, never forgetting or hiding what he represents. At the same time he extends the utmost courtesy and respect to his host environment, seeking to learn and bless rather than antagonize. Such should be the posture of Christians who are ambassadors in English classes.

A host, as I use the term here, is on "owned" territory. When we create our own surroundings, as we do when developing a church or school or creating a home study environment, we have control over that territory, and therefore can act as *hosts* towards those who enter the premises. We have chosen everything from the curriculum to the staff to the décor. We are transparent in clearly stating who we are and what we represent. On that basis, we can graciously invite others to enter of their own free will, and participate in what we have to offer. Smith and Carvill (2000), in their book *The Gift of the Stranger: Faith, Hospitality, and Foreign Language Learning,* have spoken of the foreign-language classroom as a place to extend hospitality. It is that notion that I wish to put forward here—that as hosts we can welcome language learners onto our premises, care for them, respect them, and also allow them to see us as Christ-followers.

PURPOSES PLUS PERSPECTIVES = TYPES OF ENGLISH MINISTRY

As the purposes and perspectives intersect, four types of English ministry emerge: 1) ambassador evangelism; 2) host evangelism; 3) ambassador discipleship; 4) host discipleship.

In Table 1 we see the four quadrants, with examples of English ministries in each. In the remainder of this chapter we will look at each ministry type separately, with a view to discovering what effective ministry might look like.

In each category I first present what I consider to be hallmarks of effectiveness, and then share a story—an example of that type of English ministry. Finally, I present an analysis of the ministry and how it could be improved. As we look at the ministry types separately, keep in mind that it is possible for a specific ministry to fit in more than one category. For example, a Christian English school may engage in both evangelism and discipleship. Or a specific ministry context may have characteristics of both ambassador and host. For the sake of looking at effectiveness in different types of ministries, however, we will look at each category as distinct from the others.

	AMBASSADOR	HOST
EVANGELISM	***Ambassador evangelism*** Examples: 1. A Christian teaching English at a secular university. 2. A Christian organization operating a secular (no Christian agenda put forward, Christian materials are not used, and non-Christians are possibly on the teaching staff alongside Christians) English school to meet a community request or need for better English-learning opportunities.	***Host evangelism*** Examples: 1. A Christian providing an English Bible study in her home for interested neighbors. 2. A Christian organization providing an overtly Christian English camp.
DISCIPLESHIP	***Ambassador discipleship*** Examples: 1. A Christian teaching English in a seminary not run by his own organization, using a curriculum that he did not choose. 2. A Christian organization invited to develop and run an English program within a nominally Christian school, following the often-secular school norms.	***Host discipleship*** Examples: 1. A Christian teaching English in a seminary run by his own organization, with freedom to create his own curriculum. 2. A Christian organization developing and operating an overtly Christian English school primarily for Christians in the community.

Table 1. Types of English ministry

AMBASSADOR EVANGELISM

This is the most obvious and common type of English ministry in so-called closed or creative access countries—those in which traditional missionary work is not freely permitted. As we saw in Chapter 2, work of this nature has been negatively labeled "Teaching English as a Missionary Language" by Pennycook and Coutand-Marin (2003), and has been roundly criticized by a few well-known scholars in the TESOL profession. Much of the criticism seems to stem not from documented cases of student harm, but from a fundamental opposition to evangelism as they understand it. Baurain (2007) states the common misperception in this way: "Believers are by definition indoctrinators; the desire to convert another is by definition disrespectful" (p. 209). In other words, a person who claims to be an evangelical Christian is thought to unduly and inappropriately seek to influence students' spiritual perspectives, even when this may not be the case.

Evangelical Christian missionaries are unlikely to escape criticism from those who are fundamentally opposed to any type of activity that could result in conversion. However, we must do all that we can to ensure that our activities are above reproach. It is with this goal in mind that I present the following hallmarks of effectiveness for this kind of ministry.

HALLMARKS OF EFFECTIVENESS

1. *Teaching well*

   Though this is important in any context, it is one of the prime witnesses of our Christian faith when we are engaged in this type of English ministry. The Bible says, "Whatever you do, work at it with all your heart, as working for the Lord, not for men" (Col 3:23). It could be argued that ambassador evangelism is the category that *most* requires appropriate training in teaching English.

2. *Selecting edifying course content*

   We must always choose course materials which will accomplish the stated goals of the course we are teaching,[7] and we may well be given course materials that must be used. But often we have some latitude in selecting topics and themes for language learning. Purgason (2009) claims that "typical

7 See more in Chapter 6 on the importance of valuing the course goals and organizing classes to meet them.

textbooks teach students the language of buying, but not charitable giving, complaining, but not necessarily praising, and apologizing, but usually not forgiving" (p. 190). By using readings and dialogues that have potential to help students relate well to others and develop as people, we simultaneously allow students to see us as individuals who care about more than language skills and foster a desire in students to consider important life issues.

Teachers coming from Western societies would also do well to investigate the possibilities of using religiously oriented materials in their ministry contexts. The stark "separation of church and state" that Westerners are accustomed to is odd and unnatural in some parts of the world. Wong (2009) says, "One might make the claim that we are in fact imposing our Western views on our students by *not* allowing space for classroom discussions of spiritual identity or religion" (p. 94).

3. *Selecting developmental teaching methods*[8]
Educators in the West typically advocate moving away from transmission approaches and embracing more constructivist, learner-centered ways of teaching. Simply memorizing content for a test is less valued than activities such as investigative group projects, student reflections on learning, and peer and self-evaluation. Though there are many parts of the world which still rely on transmission approaches, the fact that more developmental methodologies are used in many English-speaking countries sometimes means that foreign English teachers can use them even if local teachers do not. In some places there is a general understanding that learning English involves "strange" methods such as getting students out of their seats to ask each other questions, playing games, and engaging in pair or group work, and this is accepted. However, as mentioned in Chapter 2, caution is advised when introducing new methods in a traditional setting. Respect for the local ways is of utmost importance, and introducing new methods only with the blessing of those in leadership is the best way forward.

But if you are able to use developmental methods, how can these constitute ministry? Developmental methods often promote more critical thought than transmission approaches, and critical thought can lead to an ultimate search for truth. No, there is nothing overtly Christian in having students think through a problem to arrive at an answer, rather than memorizing the

8 See Chapter 6 for a fuller description of what I call "developmental teaching methods."

teacher's answer. But the thought process will better equip students to question the assumptions and beliefs they have been handed and to ultimately *choose* what they believe, rather than going through life passively accepting whatever they are told. In biblical terms, the use of developmental methodologies might be akin to plowing the ground of the "beaten" path that Jesus speaks of in the parable of the seeds and the sower (see Luke 8: 11–15). In English classes we can prepare the ground through constructivist activities, so that at some future point important truths may have a place to take root.

4. *Forming personal relationships*
   Ambassador evangelism through English teaching has often viewed the personal relationships that are formed as *the* ministry side of teaching English. It is, indeed, the result that we most commonly look for when we investigate the effectiveness of English ministries. There are contexts in which personal connections can only be pursued with great caution. And I emphasize again that local laws and norms must be respected. However, in any context relationships on some level are possible, and relationship building should be seen as a goal in effective English ministry. English teachers may be able to visit the homes of the children they teach. They may be able to invite adult students to their homes for informal conversations. They may be able to host study groups on topics such as "comparing religions" or "the purpose of life" or "building a good marriage" for those who are interested. Sending organizations and local norms will dictate the possibilities and constraints on such activities. But the old teaching motto, "Teach all, reach some, touch one" can encourage us. Touching one is worth it.

Story: Teaching English in a Muslim elementary school

While working in Asia developing a teacher education program, I also volunteered at a local Muslim elementary school. In my initial visit to the school I clearly stated that I was a Christian, but that my intent was to respect the Muslim orientation of the school. I was then invited to teach English there, and for a period of three years I taught an average of three to four days per week, one to two hours each time.

From the beginning, it was the hardest teaching I have ever done. I worked with third through sixth graders who seemingly had learned largely through rote repetition. Early in my time there, the depth of the rote repetition orientation became clear to me through a particular incident. I was endeavoring to teach the pronouns "he" and "she"—difficult for my students, as their language did not have gendered pronouns. I walked through the classroom tapping boys and girls on the shoulder, saying the correct pronouns. The children seemed to be trying to say the words along with me, so I felt I was making progress. Then, I pointed to my daughter at the front of the class, who was helping me teach that day. "He or she?" I asked. You can guess the response: "He or she" yelled loudly in unison. I quickly changed my intonation to make it clear, I thought, that "he" and "she" were the possible answers to this question. Still the loud chorus echo rang out: "HE or SHE!" Then it suddenly dawned on me that my students did not know the word "or" in English, so I changed that to the local language. Pointing to my daughter once again, I asked, "HE *atau* SHE?" Without a moment's pause, the excited choral response was, "HE *atau* SHE!" The children were enjoying this fun game of repetition, with nary an inkling that they were being asked a question. From then on, I realized that this teaching context would challenge many assumptions I had held about English teaching.

I had urged the school to view my classes as supplementary. I did not want them to abandon their own teaching materials, as I feared that my purely communicative activities would not prepare students for their national test. However, I soon discovered that my classes were indeed replacing the other classes, and I worried that the children weren't using any texts. Their own locally produced English workbooks contained traditional exercises in very small print on extremely thin paper. In addition, they were obviously produced for public, not Muslim school education. I wondered if perhaps the school would like materials with more modern activities and a more religious orientation.

In my previous work in Brazil we had produced a set of children's English-learning materials with the theme *God is Good.* I set about adapting this material to make it suitable for a Muslim rather than a Christian context. I showed the set to the school leadership and asked if they felt it would be appropriate for their students. They were thrilled! I am still not sure if their excitement came from the more attractive and modern look of the pages, the fact that my organization footed the bill for the materials, or the inclusion of religious content. For whatever reason though, the school was pleased with the materials, and I was able to use them there for the next two years.

The school embraced other initiatives of mine as well. We were able to hold an "English Day" at the school, with the help of a group of North American volunteers. We also had a special Thanksgiving Day, during which it seemed to me that the students were surprised to learn that Christians prayed just as they did. Other initiatives, however, were rejected. I was not allowed to take the students to my home to bake "holiday cookies," or to explain to them what Christians celebrate at Christmas time. As my time there drew to a close, I regretted not having made more connections in the village, or having spent time getting to know the children's families. However, I did witness a vast change from rote-repetition responses to critical thought. I am hopeful that some of the children I taught will be open to embracing a different future because of my time with them.

Analysis

In my work at this school I tried to teach well, but despite all my training in education and specifically in teaching English, I was unprepared for the unique challenges of that context. A goal that I pursue now is discovering what good teaching looks like in such a context and preparing others for such ministry. I did bring in edifying course content, and I also used developmental methodologies. On the last hallmark of effectiveness, however, I failed. I did not establish the personal relationships that could have greatly increased the likelihood of lasting fruit from this ministry. What happened in this endeavor happens time and time again in missions: I was too busy. A ministry such as this one should be a person's main assignment, so that there is ample time to devote to teaching well and establishing relationships.

HOST EVANGELISM

Picture a book study in your own living room, where everyone is reading about the life of C. S. Lewis, using a limited English biography, and engaging in deep discussion on his philosophies and life purpose. The participants in this study are not Christians, but they have come to your home knowing that they will be learning about C. S. Lewis, whom they know is a Christian. They also know that you are a Christian. They have come willingly, even eagerly, and are engaged in fascinating, life-changing discussions. Could English ministries get any better than this? Not really! In some contexts there may be legal or other contextual factors limiting this type of work. But in a great many parts of the world this type of English teaching would be just fine.

Why does this not happen more often? One reason is due to the difficulties of getting a student group together. It's somewhat odd to just hang a shingle outside your door saying "Book studies here every Tuesday night." It is often easier to go where the students already are, which is usually in established schools. And it is even more difficult to maintain a group over the course of several months. Dropout rates for this kind of extra-curricular study are high. However, as we will see below, there are some real attractions to host-type ministries, and Christ's kingdom would be well served if we tried to learn how to do them effectively.

HALLMARKS OF EFFECTIVENESS

1. *Transparency*

   It is essential, when we are inviting people into our space, that they know exactly what they are getting themselves into. There are places where the words "Christian" and "Bible" carry cultural baggage that we may not wish to be associated with and that's fine. We may choose instead to say that we are "followers of Christ" and that the text we are using is "a story that Jesus told." But whatever language we use, we must not mislead students into thinking they have come into a secular environment, then spring religious topics on them.

   Having said this, however, transparency here applies to what transpires in the English-teaching lesson and context, not to everything about the teacher's life or belief system. Robison (2009) states regarding the issue of teacher transparency that "personal control over information flowing out from oneself is essential to psychological wholeness" (p. 261). Sane people do not go around telling everyone everything that they think and feel. In many situations it would be disrespectful and intrusive for us to tell others that we want them to know the Lord. That information is often the opposite of transparent: it leads people to wrong understandings and fosters confusion.

2. *Knowledge of subject*

   Sometimes the subject being taught is English, pure and simple. If that is the case, then the teacher should have training in teaching English, and should be qualified to bear the label "English teacher." But in what is known as *content-based language instruction,* a growing trend in English teaching, students learn another subject through a foreign language such as English. Because the medium of instruction is English, they are learning English as well as learning the course content. Content-based instruction is most often linked to academic settings, as students learn math, science, or even theology through English. But the concept can apply equally well to classes that have been used as outreach in missions for many years, such as cooking classes and Bible studies. In this type of English ministry, depending on the specific content involved, the teacher may be more a content teacher than a language teacher, and as such needs to be very knowledgeable about the course content. However, the unique challenges in teaching content for the purpose of language learning should not be underestimated, and teachers of such classes would do well to also have training in TESOL.

3. *Quality*

   Why would those who do not know Christ want to come to something that is Christian? Often, the answer is quality. Perhaps this means top-quality materials. Perhaps it means effective and dependable organization. Perhaps it means highly proficient English speakers to interact with. Whatever draws students in, it often has something to do with quality.

   A word of caution here: while quality is important, it should be characterized more by "doing our best" than by "having the most." Take, for instance, a scenario in which a Christian English school has host evangelism as a goal, but is competing with several other local English schools. The Christian school may have more accessibility to funds and may be able to have newer textbooks, a better computer room, and a lower fee. Students may love this, but it could also result in community or professional distrust as the "foreigners" take students (and therefore income) away from other local English schools. We need to move cautiously, always looking ahead to the potential ramifications of our actions and being sure to look not only at our impact on individuals, but also on the community.

Story: An English camp

Our English school in Brazil developed a yearly English camp.[9] It was a five-day event that entailed about five months of work, and I was always exceedingly glad when it was over. Our combined Brazilian and expatriate teaching staff took over more of the leadership responsibilities with each successive year, and I came to feel that there was actually more Christian leadership training taking place than there was evangelism.

9 See Appendix C for information about developing this type of English camp.

For each camp we had a group of North American Christians come to help. These were volunteers who were usually not teachers. They would come to Brazil for two weeks, receiving some training before the camp and having some sightseeing afterwards. During the camp, these volunteers were conversation partners, cabin helpers, group leaders for sports and games, and workshop leaders. The daily workshops were the core teaching time of the camp. The workshops were on all sorts of topics: American and Canadian culture, writing greetings in English, music, cooking, sports, crafts, games, Bible studies, and much more. Camp participants signed up for the workshops they wanted to attend, with a few English-level restrictions. We took care to assign workshop topics in which the North American volunteers felt they had a certain level of expertise. They were always required to prepare their own workshops during the precamp training time, under my guidance and direction. Thus, they were not teaching "packaged" material, but were teaching material that they had developed and taken ownership of. Though the workshops did not usually focus on the English language, the fact that they were conducted in English, by volunteers who could not speak Portuguese, meant that English was used and practiced. Vocabulary worksheets on the topic of the workshop were often used, facilitating the acquisition of topic-specific language.

People from our city knew that our school was Christian and likely assumed that our camp was Christian as well. Many of those in attendance at our camps were students in our programs and were Christians. We did, however, also attract non-Christians or those who were nominally Catholic or Protestant. We had no preaching at our camps. Instead, campers were exposed to Christianity through "cabin chats" each evening—our version of devotionals. These devotionals always linked to the humorous skits that we put on in the evenings about culture and language, building on themes that campers had heard earlier.

I was not entirely happy with our level of transparency at these camps. One year, for instance, our marketing manger felt that we did not need to advertise as a Christian camp. He felt that the mention of Bible studies and singing choruses would adequately convey the point. For those in our city, this may have been true. However, that year a prominent businessman from another city decided to come to our camp. He nearly left after a few hours at the camp, when he sensed that it was indeed Christian. We apologized for our lack of transparency and urged him to stay and participate only in the activities he was comfortable with.

He ended up having a very good time, even lamenting that our school was not in his city. However, he did not return the following year.

Analysis

We did have subject-level knowledge and transparency in how we represented the training of our staff. The North American volunteers conducted workshops on topics which they were knowledgeable about and were never represented as English teachers. Trained English teachers, both Brazilians and expatriates, oversaw the team activities and evening events, which included English-learning activities. The North American short-term volunteers were provided a crash course in how to help someone learn English during the precamp training days. This did not make them English teachers, but it did make them more capable coaches and conversation partners. The camps also exhibited quality. Our great Brazilian and expatriate staff capably fulfilled their various roles, leading campers and North American volunteers alike to comment on how organized and professional it was.

However, we did not do well in the area of transparency in marketing. Some may look at the case of the man who didn't appreciate the Christian nature of the camp, and conclude, "He wouldn't have come had he known it was Christian. Because he didn't know, he came, and heard about Christ." The problem with this perspective is twofold. First, it assumes that God needs our trickery in order to bring people to Himself. This is obviously not true. Jesus said, "No one can come to me unless the Father who sent me draws him" (John 6:44). God will draw individuals to Himself. He chooses to use us, but certainly does not need us to seduce people into hearing the gospel. Second, it does not consider the long-term negative impact on the man or those he may have talked to about the incident. We often suffer from shortsightedness in ministry, looking only at our success stories and failing to see those we may actually drive further from Christ with our methods.

AMBASSADOR DISCIPLESHIP

This type of English ministry may be the least common. We find it when we are placed as English teachers in situations that are Christian in theory, but are possibly not as committed to Christian principles and ideals as we would want them to be, or not as open to Christianity in the English classroom as we would choose. In other words, we are teaching English in a Christian setting, but it leaves a lot to be desired from a spiritual point of view. Imagine that a passionate, young, short-term missionary is hired to teach English at a national Christian school abroad only to discover that the school leadership is corrupt, the students claim to be Christians but are rude and self-serving, and the English textbook portrays values which are decidedly un-Christian. What can be done? What does effective English ministry look like in such contexts?

1. *Teaching well*
   Again, this is crucial when we are ambassadors—even in Christian contexts. This is one key way through which we earn the right to have a say in other issues that we might want to change. Teachers in such contexts should have training appropriate to the level and content that they are teaching. (See Chapter 4 for a discussion on levels of training needed for various types of teaching.)
2. *Selecting course content for spiritual growth*
   As stated previously, we must always choose course materials which will accomplish the stated goals of the course we are teaching. And in school contexts, teachers are usually given texts that must be used. But often we still have some latitude in selecting topics and themes for language learning. And in a school labeled as Christian, whether it is very Christian or not, there is often no objection to the use of overtly Christian materials. Care should be taken to thoughtfully consider what kinds of materials used in the English class could effectively promote spiritual growth. For example, studying yet another scripture passage may cause sixth-grade students to feel like they are getting a double dose of "boring Bible class" instead of causing spiritual growth. Reading about the life of Jim Elliot, on the other hand, may cause them to want to know more about the Christian life.
3. *Selecting developmental teaching methods*
   In the earlier description of ambassador evangelism, I explained the concept of developmental teaching methods. Such methods are crucial in discipleship contexts as well, especially when teaching children. Children in Christian schools are often operating on a borrowed faith—one which may even be weak and underdeveloped in their parents. It is therefore important to equip them with critical thinking skills so that they can eventually come to question, understand, and own their faith. In some schools they may be developing such skills in other content classes, but there are Christian school

settings in many parts of the world that are still very transmission-dominated and which may not actively develop critical thinking skills.

4. *Forming meaningful mentoring relationships*
   Though we teach many, we usually have opportunities to mentor only a few. The mistake sometimes made in Christian contexts is thinking that someone else must be doing this—the parents, pastor, or Sunday school teacher. Surely it does not fall to the English teacher! But if the English teacher is willing, there are *always* students in the class who are not being mentored by anyone else, and a personal touch on their lives, even for a short time, may mean the difference between a vibrant faith and an abandoned faith. English teachers are often encouraged in such contexts to provide tutoring and one-on-one help after school. Why not make that time into a time of discipleship? You are likely free to pray with the student, to hear his or her concerns, and to offer support and help. You have the freedom of bringing in scriptural principles that apply to daily life situations. You may be one of the few *active* Christians that a child has had a personal relationship with.

Story: A Catholic university in Spain

Anna was in Spain as a short-term missionary. Through a friend of a friend she heard that a local Catholic university was looking for a native English speaker[10] to help out in an English class. She had no training in teaching English, but thought that she was just going to help the regular teacher, so it would be okay. Her field leader thought this might be a good opportunity to make contacts, so Anna decided to take the job.

As it turned out, Anna was assigned student conversation groups at a different time than the regular English class, so the teacher was not in the classroom. When she asked the teacher what she should do in class, making it clear that she was not a trained English teacher, the teacher said, "Just talk about something—movies, your country . . . anything!" Anna prepared some questions about popular movies for the first conversation session. The students' English level was lower than she had anticipated, and her Spanish was not yet very fluent, but they

10 The problem with the "native speaker fallacy" was addressed in Chapter 2. Though requests for "native speakers" are still abundant, we should do whatever we can in local contexts to promote the understanding that proficient speakers are needed and that having English as the first language is not necessary for effective teaching.

had a good time. The students spoke quite a bit in Spanish, and she wondered how effective the class was as an English class, but she established good rapport.

Throughout the semester Anna brought in topics mostly about popular culture. They listened to music and talked about the latest trends and movies. The students seemed interested in these topics. Though she considered introducing more spiritual topics, she was afraid that there might be something wrong with that, though she wasn't sure what.

One day one of Anna's star students was quiet and sullen during class. Anna asked if she wanted to stay after class and talk. She did, and that was the beginning of weekly meetings with a young woman who had just found out that her mom had cancer. The student said that she believed the Bible, so each week Anna brought scripture verses about God's love and comfort. They worked together on understanding the verses in English, and one day the student came in with a bilingual Spanish/English Bible, beaming over her discovery, exclaiming, "Now I can know Bible better!" By the end of the semester, when Anna was due to return home, she had been able to bring her student to church with her once and introduce her to other Spanish Christians.

ANALYSIS

Anna did her best to teach well. She made no claims of being an English teacher, and did the best she could in the context in which she found herself, thrust into a role that she had not bargained for. Anna's story highlights why it is advisable for mission organizations to have TESOL support personnel that missionaries like Anna can call on. Anna was not equipped with English-teaching methodology, but intuitively knew that bringing in questions for discussion on popular culture might work well in a university setting, and she was right. Her methodology was appropriate for her context. Anna exhibited wonderful sensitivity when she noticed that a student was suffering and offered to meet with her. Anna mentored this student, and because of this mentorship, we can certainly say that ministry took place during this English-teaching assignment. However, Anna may have missed an opportunity to accomplish more. She perhaps could have demonstrated her value and respect for the Spanish language and culture by asking her students to help her with Spanish and even by providing the young woman she mentored with a bilingual Bible. In addition, she did not bring in topics which may have led to spiritual growth for more students. If she was unsure about the appropriateness of using Bible-based materials, she could have either asked the teacher if it was okay, or brought in less controversial but still thought-provoking topics such as bioethics or social responsibility. In short, she did not try to have an impact on her students' thinking through more purposeful topics, even though she was given great latitude for content selection.

HOST DISCIPLESHIP

This can be the most overtly Christian teaching environment of the four. In this type of context we are *hosts,* that is, we control the environment (the school, church, or home setting), and we are working with those who are already Christians, and are presumably eager to grow in their faith. Sometimes we find this type of context in situations designed specifically for spiritual growth, and other times we may need to introduce the concept of spiritual growth, because others have viewed it as "just an English class."

HALLMARKS OF EFFECTIVENESS

1. *Content knowledge and teaching skill*
   Whatever the designated content, be it Bible, English, relationships, or study skills, the teacher must be knowledgeable in it. The teacher should also have appropriate teaching skills for the age group involved. Unfortunately, we sometimes cut corners on qualifications a little more easily when operating within friendly territory. Perhaps we don't have a qualified English teacher for the seminary English class, so any available English speaker can do it. Or maybe our church wants to start an English after-school club for kids. We don't have anyone with any background in teaching English to children, but we'll give it a try. Once again, here is a case in which an on-call TESOL expert in the organization could be of great assistance.
2. *Selecting course content for spiritual growth*
   In this context, we really do have a home-court advantage. We are free to choose content, and we should make every effort to choose content which meets English-learning goals but which also results in spiritual growth. I groan inwardly when I walk into a seminary English classroom and hear no mention of spiritual issues. This is a travesty. In contexts where people are beginning their preparation for ministry having little Bible knowledge or exposure to the world of Christianity, we dare not waste time in English classes talking about issues that do not contribute to spiritual development. Course content suitable for discipleship through English classes could include

cultural differences in the interpretation of scriptures, what servant leadership looks like in the local cultural context, and of course Bible study itself. (See Appendix E for resources appropriate for such settings.)

3. *Selecting developmental teaching methods*
   The concept of developmental teaching methods was explained earlier. The mistake often made is thinking that once people are Christians, and especially if they have chosen a course of study such as seminary education, they are already fully committed to learning, and all we need to provide is content. Nothing could be further from the truth! Such students usually do have a deep-seated desire to learn, but sometimes that desire is so deep as to appear dead and buried during class time. Some students have only experienced school as memorizing information and writing it back to the teacher on tests. Many have not developed critical thought patterns, a skill that is absolutely essential in ministry. For these reasons, the English teacher in Christian schools, churches, or seminaries should actively use methodology which utilizes student involvement and decision making, and which fosters learner autonomy and responsibility.
4. *Forming meaningful mentoring relationships*
   In the previous ambassador discipleship context, I suggested that just mentoring one is sufficient for effective ministry. In our "home-court" context, however, one is not enough. I have never yet seen a Christian school, seminary, or church setting where there were enough qualified mentors to go around. Though this is often not seen as part of the English teacher's job, it could and should be in host discipleship.

Story: A Bible school English class

Nathan had traveled to Africa once during college and loved it. So after graduation, when a teaching job had not come along, he accepted a missionary friend's invitation to teach English at their Bible school in Mozambique. He was not an English teacher, but he had studied to be a science teacher, and felt that he could probably wing the English part. His first visit to the classroom was a shock, when he discovered forty students, mostly male, sitting in rows, waiting for class to begin. Nathan had a textbook to use, but the students did not. Instead, he had to write information on the board, which the students diligently copied in their notebooks. Upon discovering that some Portuguese/English bilingual

Bibles had been donated to the school and that he was free to use these in his class, Nathan quickly switched to the Bible as his textbook.

With the textbook problem solved, Nathan proceeded to think about how he could organize his classes. He settled on providing questions for Bible passages, then organizing students in small groups to read the passages aloud and answer the questions together. This worked reasonably well, and the students seemed to enjoy the interaction. Occasionally it seemed that they were speaking more in their tribal languages and in the national language of Portuguese than in English, but when he reminded them to use English they tried to comply. Nathan actually found that he enjoyed the enthusiastic multilingual conversations that emerged when students were reflecting on a passage of scripture together, and he even learned some local words as a result. As time went on, Nathan tried to incorporate some variety into his classes. He had students act out parables, translate passages, and sing English choruses.

After a couple of months, Nathan decided to start an English sports club. He would get together and play basketball or soccer with interested students after class on Thursdays. When they were sweaty and hot after the game, they would sit around talking and sharing—sometimes for an hour or more. Nathan got to know a few of the students really well through this informal sharing time, and found that he was eventually able to ask some deeper questions about their call to the ministry and their struggles in living the Christian life. He didn't really know much more about the Christian life than some of his students, but as a Christian brother and peer, he was able to listen and pray.

At the end of the year, Nathan was pretty sure his students had not learned much about English grammar. However, he felt that he did help them develop something they needed: Christian and Bible vocabulary in English. But he felt even better about the level of relationship he had developed with a few of his students. Nathan is under no illusion that he is an English teacher, but he does feel he had an effective ministry through an English class.

Analysis

Nathan is right: he *did* have an effective ministry with young African men preparing for spiritual leadership. Like Anna, he took a difficult teaching situation and made the most of it. The learning activities he came up with are good—certainly more developmental in nature than lecturing, and effective in the context. His lack of training in English teaching limited his resources both in content and in methodology. Once again, access to a TESOL consultant in his organization could have been very helpful in offering Nathan some additional ideas and materials. Nathan's interaction with the students after his sports club may not have been exactly mentorship, as it was informal conversation between peers, but it was nevertheless what Nathan could offer. The lasting friendships formed may well be an ongoing source of encouragement for the students in Mozambique and for Nathan.

CONCLUSION

The four types of English ministry discussed in this chapter provide a general understanding of both the purposes of English ministry and the perspectives from which we operate as English teachers. As previously stated, these types may overlap or not be as clear-cut in real ministry contexts. But these definitions can provide us with a basis on which to evaluate the effectiveness of our English ministries.

DISCUSSION AND APPLICATION

1. In the section "What English ministry is not," two overarching principles are provided for English ministry. What are these?
2. Consider the following English-ministry scenarios. For each, decide which of the four types of English ministry it is. Then write a brief description of what the teacher might endeavor to accomplish, according to the "hallmarks of effectiveness" for that type of ministry.
   a. A missionary in El Salvador is invited to teach English in a local elementary Catholic school.
   b. A short-termer goes to China to teach English in a university.
   c. Seminary students in Lebanon take a course in academic reading with a local Christian English teacher.
   d. A missionary in Japan provides a class in American cooking in her home.
3. Consider an English ministry that you are familiar with. Describe the context and tell which type of ministry it is. Evaluate the effectiveness of this ministry.
4. Imagine that you have been asked by a mission agency to set up an English ministry in a country of your choice. Describe the context, what type of ministry you would set up, and how you would ensure that the ministry was effective.

CHAPTER 4

ENGLISH TEACHERS WITH INTEGRITY: THREE REQUIREMENTS

In Chapter 3 we focused on types of English ministries. Now we want to look at the people who carry out these ministries and what they need in order to be effective. I will address three skill areas that I believe are needed in those who claim to minister for Christ through English teaching: 1) professional skills: the knowledge and abilities needed to teach English effectively 2) relational skills: appropriate teacher dispositions and contextual/cultural understanding and 3) ministry skills: understanding what constitutes appropriate evangelism and discipleship within an English-teaching context. Then I will close the chapter with a call to position ourselves as learners rather than experts as we cross cultures in ministry.

It is important to note at the outset that I put forward a view that both native and nonnative English speakers can contribute effectively to English ministries. My own dissertation research with native and nonnative English-speaking teachers in Brazil and Indonesia (Dormer, 2006) and the work of many other TESOL researchers confirms that both can be excellent English teachers and may actually bring different and complementary teaching skills to English-learning programs. We are overlooking a vast resource of professionally trained personnel by seeing English ministry as something that only those born in English-speaking countries can do. It is true that the stories I am using in this book often either feature native English speakers or do not mention nationality, thus perhaps encouraging the assumption that I am talking about native English speakers. But note that Brazilian English teachers figure prominently in two of the case studies in this book. My examples are either actual case studies or composite sketches of known ministry activities, and nonnative English-speaking teachers are not yet prominent in these types of ministries. I hope that in the future they will be. But for now, please remember as you read through this chapter and the remainder of this book that it would be ideal if our future English ministries featured teachers from countries such as Taiwan, Poland, and Argentina working alongside teachers from places such as Australia, Canada, and Ireland.

PROFESSIONAL SKILLS

Do you remember Bill from Chapter 1? He was struggling in his ministry assignment as an English teacher in an Asian university. He may have been prepared with ministry and relational skills, but he did not possess the professional skills needed for the job; he was not an English teacher. To review, let's look again at the four main skill areas in English teaching, which were introduced in Chapter 1. We can say that these are the *professional skills* that are needed in teaching English:

1. Communicative competence: skill in using English
2. Linguistic knowledge: understanding the rules of English
3. Theoretical knowledge: understanding English-language learning
4. Methodological competence: skill in English teaching

When those engaged in or preparing for overseas ministry begin to understand the field of TESOL, they sometimes ask, "What kind of preparation does a person need to teach English?" The answer to this question depends on many factors, including the type of English teaching that will be done, the formal and informal learning experiences of the teacher, and the amount of support provided by the organization. So in order to shed some light on this topic, I will devote considerable space to the issue of professional preparation in this chapter.

SOURCES OF ENGLISH-TEACHING COMPETENCY

Misconceptions about the professional preparation needed to teach English usually stem from one of two extremes. The first extreme is the idea that no specific skills are needed. This is the misconception that was addressed in Chapter 1. The point was made that there are indeed specific skills needed to teach English, beyond the ability to speak it. But another misconception lies at the opposite extreme: that the only way to acquire the skills needed to teach English is to earn a degree in TESOL. Though I do believe that all English teachers would benefit from at least a certificate-level course in TESOL, we should also understand that the four skill areas above can be acquired in diverse ways. People can pick up some theoretical knowledge about the process of language acquisition, for example, by studying a foreign language. They may have gained some methodological competence by having a teacher in high school who used some great techniques that they still remember. There are also those whom we might label "natural-born teachers"—people who just seem to do a great job in the classroom despite a lack of formal teacher education.

A word about experience. There are individuals who actively study the craft of teaching and become better teachers the longer they are in the classroom. However, there are others who do not necessarily learn by doing. Some such individuals can be more dangerous than novice teachers, because they think of themselves as veterans who know how to teach and may not consider the possibility that they may have been doing it with minimal effectiveness all these years. Whether or not experience alone has made one a better teacher depends on the individual. In my experience working with novice and veteran, trained and untrained teachers, I have concluded that *trained* teachers sometimes improve more through experience than *untrained* teachers. They have theoretical knowledge to pull from when they encounter difficulties in the classroom, and additionally often know where to turn for advice. Untrained teachers sometimes lack both knowledge and resources for using difficulties to improve their teaching.

Take a moment to look at Table 2. Here we see some of the possible ways in which individuals may acquire language and teaching skills. This chart suggests the likelihood of the development of these competencies and knowledge bases through the means listed. For example, by virtue of being a native speaker we could predict that communicative competence would be "high." Methodological competence for the category of native speaker, on the other hand, is "none," because a person acquires no teaching skills simply by virtue of being a native speaker of any language.

The "ways to acquire competencies and knowledge" are cumulative. For example, a short certificate course in TESOL may only develop communicative competence to a "low" level. But if an individual is already "high" in communicative competence, due to having learned English as a second language to a high level, for example, then communicative competence is still high.

The predictions in this chart are based on my experience in working with language teachers in several different contexts and my knowledge of general and specific educational programs. These are generalizations and should be used only as a guide. Individuals and programs may fall outside the norm in any category.

WAYS TO DEVELOP COMPETENCIES AND KNOWLEDGE

COMMUNICATIVE COMPETENCE	LINGUISTIC KNOWLEDGE	THEORETICAL KNOWLEDGE	METHODOLOGICAL COMPETENCE
English as a first language (being a native English speaker)			
High	Low	None	None
English as a second (or additional) language			
Low to high (Depending on level of mastery)	Low to high (High if grammar was learned in English classes)	None to low	None to low (May be higher if taught using good techniques)
Learning by studying another language			
None (No competence in English)	Low to medium	None to low	None to low (May be higher if taught using good techniques)
English-medium K–12 or college education in English			
Medium to high	Low to medium	None	None to low
Degree in education			
None	None	None to low	Low to medium
Innate talent, aptitude, and ability			
None	None	None	None to medium
Short certificate in TESOL (less than 100 hours)			
Low to medium	Low	Low to medium	Low to medium
Average certificate in TESOL (100 hours or more)			
Low to medium	Low to medium	Medium to high	Medium to high
Bachelor's or master's degree in TESOL			
Medium to high	High	High	High
Experience in teaching English			
Low to high	Low to high	Low to high	Low to high

Table 2. Sources of competency development

Note: In this chart I use the term TESOL (Teaching English to Speakers of Other Languages) to talk about studies in English-language teaching. Some other terms that may be used for this are TESL (Teaching English as a Second Language), TEFL (Teaching English as a Foreign Language), and ELT (English Language Teaching). In countries where English is not a national language, similar training may have a variety of other names, such as "Letters" (the teaching of foreign languages, often focused on English).

Now, let's practice using the chart by looking at three individual teachers and creating competency profiles for them. To use the chart, we will look at each of the competency columns, searching for the individual's highest rating in each. In most categories, a continuum is given, such as "medium to high." We will then look at the unique characteristics of the individual and the particulars of their sources of learning, assigning the place on the continuum that best describes their ability or knowledge level.

To begin let's return to Bill, whom we met in Chapter 1. We looked at his level of competency in Chapter 1, but will now do so again using our chart.

BILL'S PROFILE:	
Communicative competence	*High* by virtue of being a native speaker
Linguistic knowledge	*Low* by virtue of studying a foreign language and having a K–12 education in English
Theoretical knowledge	*None*
Methodological competence	*Low* by virtue of general education and aptitude

Next, we will look at the profile of Lorena, a very fluent Bolivian who teaches at a private English school. She has a BA in Psychology, followed by a short certificate course in TESOL, which included a little second language acquisition theory, but focused mostly on methodology.

LORENA'S PROFILE:	
Communicative competence	*High* by virtue of learning English as an additional language and taking English-medium college courses
Linguistic knowledge	*Medium* by virtue of learning English as an additional language
Theoretical knowledge	*Low* by virtue of a short certificate in TESOL
Methodological competence	*Medium* by virtue of a short certificate in TESOL

Finally, we will look at the profile of Suyi, a less fluent but well-educated Korean English teacher. Suyi earned a bachelor's degree in English Education and Literature, and has taught English in a Korean high school for the past five years.

SUYI'S PROFILE:	
Communicative competence	*Medium* by virtue of being an English learner
Linguistic knowledge	*High* by virtue of having a BA in TESOL
Theoretical knowledge	*High* by virtue of having a BA in TESOL
Methodological competence	*High* by virtue of having a BA in TESOL and teaching experience

How can such profiles be useful? As we saw in Chapter 3, English ministries can take many different forms and require different skills. Very different competency levels are needed, for example, to be a conversation partner or to design an English program. We will now look at another chart which again looks at the four skill areas, but this time suggests how English-ministry activities correlate with these areas.

ACTIVITIES IN ENGLISH MINISTRIES

We have seen through Bill's experience in Chapter 1 that teaching English in a university classroom setting normally requires all four of the skills, to a fairly high level. But English ministries occur in many different types of settings. Are high levels in all competencies always required? The answer is no. As we can see in Table 3, there are many ways in which English is used in ministry outside of the traditional classroom environment.

At the top of the chart we find a description of someone who is in a leadership position where English ministry is concerned. This person is creating programs, designing curricula, and supervising teachers. Such a person needs a high level of skill in each of the four areas. Looking at Table 2, we can say that this person should ideally have a bachelor's or master's degree in TESOL. If the personnel that we have to work with are Bill, Lorena, and Suyi (see their profiles above), Suyi would come the closest to being qualified for this job. Further down the chart, we see a person who is assisting a language learner as a conversation partner. This person does not need a master's degree in TESOL. Ideally, however, he or she does have some background in TESOL, and can draw on some understanding of language and methodology in an effort to help English learners in their development. Both Lorena and Bill could do this job well.

Types of English-Ministry Activities

Communicative Competence	Linguistic Knowledge	Theoretical Knowledge	Methodological Competence
Creating English programs, designing curriculum, supervising teachers			
High	High	High	High
Classroom English teaching, with no supervision by a TESOL expert			
High	Medium to high	Medium to high	High
Classroom English teaching, with supervision by a TESOL expert			
High	Medium to high	Low to medium	Medium to high
Assisting English-language learners as a conversation partner or tutor			
Medium to high	Medium	Low to medium	Low to medium
Leading a content-specific class in English, such as a Bible study or a cooking class			
Medium to high	Low	Low	Low
Interacting with English-language learners through informal activities such as sports, games and music (as might occur in an English camp)			
Medium to high	None to low	None to low	None

Table 3. English-ministry activities and minimum skills required

What about Bill's university job? Is he prepared for that? According to this chart no, he is not. However, if Suyi were providing expert TESOL supervision, as suggested in the third category, Bill would do better in his university teaching assignment, and Lorena would do great.

In conclusion, professional skills must be appropriate for the job. We would do well to title English-ministry activities as what they truly are, rather than calling anything done in English an "English class." Is the leader of the Bible study teaching English or teaching Bible? If the primary goal is to teach the Bible, that teacher should be called a Bible teacher, not an English teacher. If an English class is using some passages from the Bible for a reading activity, however, the class is an English class, and the teacher should be prepared as an English teacher. Is a short-term worker befriending an English learner for two weeks? That person is a conversation partner or culture learner/teacher, not an English teacher. Better labeling of activities will help us to be more transparent concerning what we are offering, and will lessen the burden on those who are not English teachers, but who are simply engaged in an activity through the medium of English.

TEACHING CHILDREN

Before moving on to talk about relational skills, I want to take a moment to consider the special professional skill set needed for teaching children. In recent years the field of Teaching English to Young Learners (TEYL) has seen unprecedented growth. As we learned in Chapter 2, school systems in many countries are promoting the teaching of English to ever-younger learners, and now in Indonesia, for example "baby classes" (English classes for children who cannot yet even speak their native language) are common.

Teaching young learners (from preschool to junior high) requires special skills in both theoretical knowledge and methodological competence. Children do not acquire additional languages in exactly the same ways as adults, and though many language-teaching methods are appropriate for both children and adults, managing a classroom of third graders and engaging them in active learning is significantly different from teaching a class of business people or university students.

It is beyond the scope of this book to address the specific issues involved in teaching young learners. I highly recommend David Paul's (2003) book *Teaching English to Children in Asia* for those who are teaching English to children. (Despite the title, I feel this book is appropriate for most cultural settings.)

More important than understanding language learning and methodology, though, is an understanding of the increased ethical vigilance required by those who teach children, especially when this teaching involves crossing cultural and religious boundaries. It is fairly easy to convince children of the rightness of the gospel, and to lead them to prayers of repentance. Just because this is doable does not necessarily mean it should be done. Parents maintain rights over what and how their children are taught, even when they do not hold the values and beliefs that we espouse. Governments usually uphold these rights, and for this reason sometimes have stricter laws about proselytizing children than adults. Governments recognize the vulnerability of children, and parents' rights and responsibilities in protecting them from those who may exploit them.

If parents or schools do not want their children exposed to the gospel we must respect that. You may recall my story in Chapter 3 about teaching in a Muslim school. In that context I was able to plant seeds of understanding about the nature of God, specifically his goodness. I used materials to this effect with the full blessing of the school leadership. God was at work—even though I was never able to talk about Jesus Christ.

RELATIONAL SKILLS

I frequently begin new teacher education courses by sharing my own journey from a content view of teaching to a relational view of teaching. Twenty-five years ago as a young teacher in possession of a new master's degree in teaching English as a foreign language, my first job was in a divided skills (teaching reading, writing, speaking, and listening as separate classes) program at a university in Canada. During my first semester I taught four sections of writing, and viewed myself as a "teacher of writing." I wanted to be the best writing teacher ever. It was not long, however, before I realized that you can't really teach language skills in isolation. I needed to include reading, grammar, and even speaking and listening, in order for my writing classes to be effective. And so I broadened my self-description to "teacher of English." With a few more years under my belt, I realized that to a certain extent I was not just teaching English but was teaching language, with all its cultural and sociological implications. I began to view myself as a "teacher of language." My view of teaching had broadened from isolated skills to integrated concepts, which was a very positive evolution. But the biggest change in my self-perception as a teacher came in my fifth year, when I one day was faced with a group of students who, despite all my excellent technical teaching, were not making progress. As I prayed and studied I suddenly realized to my horror that until then I had always taught the content, not the students. A radical change in my teaching began that day, when I finally began to view myself as a "teacher of students."

Students are not passive receivers of technical information. They feel, hurt, hope, care, trust, distrust, believe, love, hate, help, scorn, gossip, laugh, and dream—and they do it all over our classrooms. Students are messy! It has sometimes been said that the difference between a good teacher and a great teacher is one student, and another one, and another one . . . whose lives are truly changed. The point being that good teachers teach classes, but great teachers teach individual students. Great teachers are usually those who motivate, inspire, and care, not necessarily those who know the most about the subject matter. I use the term "relational skill" to describe this type of teacher—one who cares deeply about, and is able to relate to, the students in his or her classroom. We will consider here two factors in relational skill: *teacher dispositions* and *understanding culture and context.*

TEACHER DISPOSITIONS

"Teaching is more about who you are than what you do" is a phrase that students in my teacher education classes have heard me say many times. The level of student motivation is a significant factor in language-learning success, and thus it is the teachers who can motivate and inspire learners who are often the most successful. These teachers may or may not use the latest language-teaching techniques. They are successful primarily because they care about their students and know how to translate that caring into group and individual encounters which motivate and equip the learner to move forward in language skill. Snow (2001) affirms that teachers must be "genuinely concerned with their students' well-being, both academically and in general," and must also "make a serious effort to understand students and meet their needs" (p. 68). Meeting students' needs does, of course, return us to the need for professional skills, as discussed above. But the point here is that learner motivation often derives from a teacher's ability to connect with students, and inspire them to be all that God has created them to be.

Fortunately, the field of education is now recognizing the crucial impact that teacher dispositions have on learning. Most teacher preparation programs in North America (and likely in many other parts of the world as well) have systems in place to guarantee that their graduates show evidence of critical teacher dispositions such as compassion, dedication, fairness, honesty, high expectations, and respect for diversity. These are all biblical values, and as such should be very evident in the classrooms of Christian English teachers.

The field of TESOL is not yet as vocal about the importance of teacher dispositions as is education in general, but our view of language teaching has definitely shifted from a technical, methodology-focused one to one which values relational qualities. The promise of a foolproof, "teacher-proof" method for language teaching has been exposed for what it is: a myth. There is no such thing as a packaged, assembly-line, sterile method. Instead, the teacher should, as a wise, caring, and capable decision maker, create a classroom climate that is conducive to learning, utilizing diverse techniques to help a specific group of unique individuals acquire language skills.

One significant change in the field of TESOL in recent decades has been the switch from teacher-centered to student-centered or learning-centered methodologies. The "Sage on the Stage," characterized by a teacher at the front of the class, often in lecture mode, is much less commonly found in effective language classrooms today than the "Guide on the Side," characterized by a teacher who walks around providing help as needed as students discover and learn. (See Don Snow's book *More Than a Native Speaker: An Introduction to Teaching English Abroad,* 2006, for an extended discussion on these two classroom-teaching perspectives.) Our understanding of language learning and teaching today generally points to the value of developing *learner autonomy:* equipping learners to direct their own language learning. This usually cannot be accomplished through traditional sage-type teaching. Fundamentally, teaching is all about the learner, and it can be helpful to keep in mind this very basic definition of good teaching:

Teaching = enabling someone to learn

Cross-cultural understanding

Cultural understanding is a key ingredient in the language-teaching mix. Kaining (2003) explains that, "Without a high level of cultural awareness everything which is different can be seen as weird and abnormal" and that the only way to change this perspective is to understand the "historical and cultural traditions which resulted in these differences" (pp. 97–98). Indeed, culture learning must be a significant part of preparation for any kind of cross-cultural Christian ministry, including English teaching.

Snow (2001) speaks of "learning as witness" and the open doors for friendship when we become humble learners in a new culture. Such learning begins by learning the local language. One mistake sometimes made in short-term English-teaching assignments is not requiring teachers to learn the local language. Though English teaching often does not need to be postponed until the local language is learned, as is the case with many other ministry assignments, language classes should begin upon arrival, and should not end until the teacher has at least a basic, functional command of the language. Knowledge of the local language is immeasurably helpful not only in terms of demonstrating a desire to learn from the local people, but also in terms of understanding educational practices and particular English-learning difficulties.

We also learn much about the culture when we learn the language. Fennes and Hapgood (1997) state, "The structure of a language is interdependent with patterns of thinking and, consequently, culture. Considering this, it is not only culture that shapes language but also language that shapes culture" (p. 23).

A case in point is the Indonesian word *belajar,* which can mean both "study" and "learn." For English speakers, these are two very different concepts. Something can be studied and not really learned, or something can be learned without actual study. Indonesians, on the other hand, may tend to view the two as synonymous, because the same word describes each idea in their language. Imagine the following exchange between an Indonesian English student and an English teacher who has not learned the Indonesian language:

S: Teacher, I study much last night.
T: So, did you learn anything?
S: (Student looks puzzled.) Yes, I study a lot.
T: You already said that. Now I'm asking you if you learned anything new.
S: Yes, I study.
T: But I want to know if you *learned* . . .

The miscommunication here may never be resolved, because neither teacher nor student understands the differences between the English words *study* and *learn,* and the Indonesian word *belajar.* The teacher would never comprehend the source of the student's misunderstanding and frustration, if she has not learned the Indonesian word *belajar* and its impact on how Indonesians may think about studying and learning.

As important as language learning is, it is merely the starting point for our culture learning. We must become students of the local culture, extending our learning further and deeper, until ultimately there is an abiding respect for different ways of thinking and acting. It is fairly easy to believe that you will have this kind of respect for local ways when you are excited about going abroad to an exotic field of service. It is much harder to actually muster up this respect when you are new in the culture, facing many things that just seem wrong. In the English classroom, the local culture may exert pressure at grading time, for instance. In some cultural contexts, no one fails a class, regardless of their level of learning or accomplishment. This seems very wrong to most Westerners, and is an example of what Johnston (2003) calls a "clash between what insiders believe to be the right and good thing to do and what the outsider teacher considers to be good and right" (p. 60). Allowing every student to pass the course, regardless of the quality of their work, does not sit well with those from a culture that values individual justice and reaping what you sow. How do you respect values so opposite to your own?

Two key attitudes are helpful in facing such conflicts: 1) respecting authority and 2) reserving judgment. First, we must respect those in positions of authority who have the right to determine policies and regulations. I must realize that I am the outsider, the foreigner, and I do not hold the authority to determine grading policies. Second, we must reserve judgment. This is very difficult for many Westerners to do. We are an opinionated lot, and sadly, we sometimes do not consider our miniscule cultural understanding of an issue as the red light that it should be for us in forming opinions. Reserving judgment does not mean that we agree, but it also does not mean that we disagree. It is okay, even advisable, to say and think "I just don't know" very frequently as we are sorting out the different ways of doing business that we see all around us when we move into a new culture. This is what it means to be a culture learner.

Over time we may be able to earn the right to share our perspectives on educational practices. Our ideas may filter into local thinking, planting seeds of change which may sprout years later. But our thoughts will never be heard if we do not first approach such situations, and the people involved in them, with respect and a reservation of judgment. And let's not forget the other possible outcome on any number of issues with which we at first disagree: years later we may come to understand that they got it right after all.

The development of cross-cultural understanding means that we give up the right to view our own cultural practices as always being the best. Sometimes cultural norms clearly go against biblical teaching, and thus are wrong. This is as true in our own cultures as in those that are foreign to us. But there are many, many more times when a cultural practice may seem wrong to us, but when we get right down to it, there is no clear biblical case to be made against it. "First, remove the log from your own eye" (Matt 7:5) would seem to be the most appropriate response when faced with many if not most cultural differences.

Missionary English teachers need good relational skills. These skills begin with appropriate teacher dispositions, such as those listed above. We then need to add to the basic dispositions cross-cultural understanding, a perspective which can be seeded prior to service, but must grow to maturity on the job. As Christians, the Bible is our ultimate guide in relating to others, whether inside or out of the classroom. Paul points us in the right direction with his list of the fruit of the Spirit: love, joy, peace, patience, kindness, goodness, faithfulness, gentleness, and self-control (Gal 5:22–23). It is difficult to imagine a better relational skill set for teaching English cross-culturally.

MINISTRY SKILLS

Many non-Christian teachers have excellent professional skills. Many non-Christian teachers have excellent relational skills. It is the *ministry skills* of Christian English teachers which set us apart from other teachers. We have already discussed in Chapter 3 some of the specific ministry activities that may be used in English teaching, such as the use of edifying materials and engagement in mentorship. In this section, we want to look not at the activities, but at the ministry skill set that is needed by teachers in order to carry out these activities.

I will not address here fundamental skills that all Christians should have, such as regular times of Bible reading and prayer and the ability to explain the basic tenets of the Christian faith. Rather, I will focus on three skills which might possibly be neglected in ministry preparation when the assignment is "just teaching English": 1) an understanding of theology and religion, 2) the ability to pursue ministry, and 3) the ability to mentor.

AN UNDERSTANDING OF THEOLOGY AND RELIGION

I once worked in Brazil with a short-term English teacher who did not know that Catholicism was a Christian faith—a significantly detrimental knowledge gap in a predominantly Catholic country. I worked with another student desiring to minister to Muslims who was surprised to discover that "Arab" and "Muslim" were not the same thing. Many people today know very little about world religions. Many Christians do not have clear concepts of broader faith-related issues, either. Some university students seem to have had very little contact with the concept of *worldview.* Others confuse terms such as *ethics, theology,* and *morality.* All this to say that we cannot assume that Christians going overseas as English teachers will have sufficient knowledge to engage intelligently in conversations about theology and religion simply by virtue of calling themselves Christians.

Conversations on religion, theology, and ethics emerge frequently in English classrooms. People across the globe are curious about these topics and will often relish the opportunity to discuss or debate such issues with a foreigner. When topics related to religion and values come up naturally in or out of class, within legal boundaries, English teachers should have the background knowledge necessary to fully engage in these conversations, speaking God's truths.

Those preparing for or already involved in English ministries may want to use the following questions as a starting point, to see if they have adequate knowledge and understanding for their context in the areas of theology and religion:

1. Can you describe in some detail the dominant religious beliefs and practices?
2. Can you compare and contrast these religious practices with Christian beliefs and practices?
3. Can you explain the theological reasons for the differences between the two sets of beliefs and practices?
4. Do you know the approach that local Christians use when telling others about the gospel, and why that approach is used?
5. Do you know the main arguments against Christianity in your context? Do you know how local Christians respond to these arguments?

AN UNDERSTANDING OF HOW TO PURSUE MINISTRY

It is not a given that ministry will happen simply because we place a Christian teacher in an English-teaching assignment. Sometimes, English teachers are sent out without clear goals of what they should endeavor to accomplish in terms of ministry. Sometimes they only have one idea of how ministry could happen. If that one thing proves impossible, they have no other ideas, and so ministry does not happen. In other cases, teachers are too shy, too bold, or too culture shocked, all of which can derail ministry.

An English teacher in ministry needs an understanding of what forms ministry could take, knowledge of the constraints of the local context, and the willingness and ability to work at making the English-teaching assignment *ministry*. This is often easier said than done. A short-termer on his very first stint teaching overseas may find himself overwhelmed with lesson planning, language learning, and culture shock, and indeed have no time or energy to think about the ministry side of what he is doing. Both individual teachers and their sending organizations need to anticipate this problem and try to reduce the difficulties inherent in pursuing ministry as an English teacher. Lighter teaching and studying loads coupled with mentorship may provide the teacher with the conditions necessary for developing a real ministry.

One thing that can help is simply having a list of possible ministry options. The following activities have been mentioned in Chapter 3, but are provided again here. The first activity on the list can always be done, no matter how closed the country. Teachers can go down the list, adding those activities which are feasible in their contexts.

Ministries within the context of English teaching:

The list is arranged from those which can be done in all contexts to those which may not be possible in some contexts. A teacher should obey local laws and stay within school guidelines when choosing ministry activities.

1. Pray for your students and for God's blessing on the school and its leaders.
2. Get to know some of your students individually. Find out what they feel they need in order to pursue their goals, and meet any needs that you are able to meet. Take every opportunity to show that you genuinely care about them.
3. Tell your students about yourself. Include the fact that you are a Christian. Share your life story as the context allows.
4. Use developmental teaching methods;[11] in other words, use methods which help the students develop as people and which help them engage with topics and ideas rather than simply memorizing content.
5. Offer secular activities outside of class (e.g., a cooking class, a book study, mentorship) to help meet students' felt needs and to build relationships.
6. Use life-building topics in class (e.g., gratitude, courage, hope, good relationships) for readings, dialogues, and discussion.
7. Use religious topics in class (e.g., the meaning of life, different views of God, life after death).
8. Offer Christian activities outside of class (e.g., a Bible study, discipleship).

As a teacher begins a ministry through the teaching of English, it is important that she be accountable to someone for the ministry outcome. Most ministries are less effective than they could be if there is no system of accountability, and English ministries are no different. However, those to whom the English teacher is accountable must be well aware of *how* English teaching can be ministry. Asking the English teacher how many converts she had after a year of ministry flies in the face of much of what is being put forward in this book as effective English ministry. However, questions about methodologies, relationships with students, and materials and topics used in the classroom are appropriate. When both the English teacher and her supervisors understand what good English ministry can look like in a given context, then there can be

11 See Chapter 6 for more about developmental teaching methods.

appropriate accountability, and the likelihood that English ministry will be effective is increased.

An Ability to Mentor

A final ministry skill needed by English teachers is the ability to mentor. Ministry through English teaching will often be characterized by special relationships with a few students. Let me state again that every precaution should be taken to ensure that any special relationships that develop are completely ethical in both practice and appearance, and appropriate within the school context. Cross-gender mentorship is ill advised in most cases. Also it is sometimes best for mentorship to take place *after* a student is no longer in the class, lest there be any accusation of favoritism in assigning grades.

Mentorships develop in a number of ways, and may be called any number of things including friendship. What I am calling mentorship here is a relationship in which a mentor helps a mentee to grow or develop in some way. In an English-ministry context, sometimes such relationships emerge from tutoring sessions. At other times students may have a special need or interest which they ask the English teacher for help with, such as filling out an application or preparing for the TOEFL (Test of English as a Foreign Language). However it happens, these special relationships often lead to opportunities to mentor and sometimes even disciple students. (See Chapter 5 for student stories showcasing mentorship ministries.)

Those in English ministry need to be equipped with the confidence, skills, and materials needed for effective mentorship. Young people may lack confidence that they could mentor someone. They may view mentorship as "providing answers"—which they don't have. But mentorship is really more about asking guiding questions, listening, and asking more questions than anything else. One way we can help teachers prepare for English ministry is to provide them with an understanding of mentorship and with tools (such as workbooks or internet sites) for mentorship.

CONCLUSION

In this chapter we have seen three skill sets that missionary English teachers need: professional, relational, and ministerial. One problem with a skill-based view of ministry, though, is the danger in believing that our skills give us a right to go into a foreign country and teach people things. We get excited about blessing them with all the knowledge that we have, and in the process we may forget that our skill set is a foundation, not a completed building. The brick and mortar of cross-cultural ministry comes as we are willing to be co-constructors of God's work in a new place, alongside people who may think and act very differently from us. This construction cannot happen—despite our excellent foundation—without seeing ourselves as both cultural and spiritual learners.

Smith (2009) relates the parable of the Good Samaritan to culture learning. He describes the shock that the scribe, the one who asked Jesus, "Who is my neighbor?" (Luke 10:29), must have felt as the reality of Jesus' story featuring the despised Samaritan as the one to emulate really sank in.

> The scribe began by asking who else might count as his neighbor, as part of the true community of faith; he ends up receiving instruction (through a Samaritan!) on how he needs to change in order to be counted among the neighborly. Layer by layer, Jesus has mercilessly stripped away the scribe's ethnic and religious securities and superiorities. Mercilessly? Well no. For the story does end with an invitation, an invitation to humble himself and enter the topsy-turvy world of compassion given and received in recognition of mutual vulnerability, and a life of loving God so whole-heartedly that cherished boundaries are redrawn. (pp. 75–76)

Just as it was difficult for the well-educated, religiously upright scribe to see his need to become more like a Samaritan, of all people, it can be very difficult for us to enter new cultures with our degrees and certainties and maintain a willingness to humble ourselves and learn. This posture is made even more difficult by the unquestioned respect automatically conferred on Westerners in some contexts, especially those who are also educated professionals. It is easy to believe that we deserve it. Well, we don't. A significant part of our ministry must involve exploring, alongside those we serve, the multifaceted ways in which God is at work in their culture, building His kingdom by using our skills, yes, but more significantly by using our humility and our willingness to learn.

DISCUSSION AND APPLICATION

1. Using Table 2, analyze your professional skills. Develop your own profile similar to those of Bill, Lorena, and Suyi. Compare your profile to that of a colleague. How are you alike and different?
2. Using Table 3, decide which ministries you are currently suited for professionally, given your profile. Are there ministries that you would like to engage in that you are not currently equipped for? What would you need to do in order to become equipped for those ministries?
3. How would you describe the different perspectives in teaching content and teaching students?
4. Make your own list of five teacher dispositions that you feel might be most important in a particular English-ministry context. Why did you choose these dispositions?
5. Imagine that a friend of yours is going overseas to teach English. What tips would you provide for developing cross-cultural understanding?
6. Choose an English-ministry context and describe all the ministry preparation that will be needed for that context. Include any understanding of theology and religion that is important, teacher qualities needed to pursue ministry, and any mentorship skills that should be developed.
7. Analyze your particular skill set in relation to English ministries. Write your strengths and challenges in all three areas: professional, relational, and ministry. Now consider an English-ministry setting in which you might work. Are you fully equipped for working in that setting? If not, what additional development do you need?

CHAPTER 5

ENGLISH-TEACHING FORMATS: FOUR MODELS

In Chapter 3 we categorized English ministries in terms of their focus on either evangelism or discipleship, in either ambassador or host settings. In Chapter 4 we looked at the qualifications required of an individual involved in English ministry. Now in Chapter 5, we will take a closer look at the formats that English ministry can take.

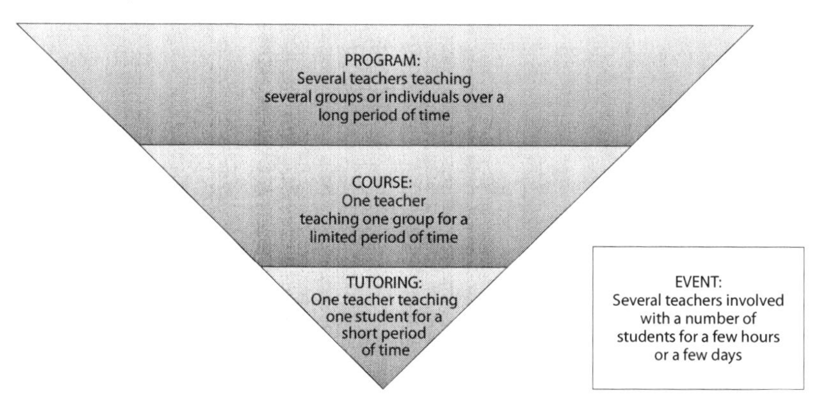

Figure 3. Models for English ministry

We will look at four different models for teaching English as ministry: programs, courses, tutoring, and events. As is shown in Figure 3, the first three models are organized from large to small, in terms of numbers of people involved and duration. The event model has been placed to the side as one that can involve significant numbers of people, but which is a one-time or very occasional occurrence. As we look at each model we will discuss what type of ministry it might be of the four types presented in Chapter 3. As we discuss these models, keep in mind the issues regarding effectiveness that were addressed in Chapters 3 and 4.

I will not repeat here, for instance, the different levels of training required for different English-ministry roles in the various models. Likewise, I will not revisit to any great extent the notion that edifying content and developmental teaching methods should be used whenever possible. Rather, this chapter seeks to outline various ways in which English ministry may be structured, providing ideas and suggestions for different models.

PROGRAMS

We begin at the top by discussing English-ministry programs. A program, as I use the term here, describes a language study context that encompasses more than a course or class. The Christian English school that I developed in Brazil was successful more because of the total language-learning environment that it offered than its individual English classes. The program concept of English ministries would most likely be a *host* initiative. Often *evangelism* is the main goal, but *discipleship* may be an additional goal. Our school in Brazil sought to attract both Christians and non-Christians, providing a variety of choices regarding content and classes so that students could feel comfortable at many different levels of spiritual interest and development. A program may be an actual English school, as it was in the Brazilian context I describe here. But a church, a seminary, or perhaps even a loosely organized group of individuals could also run a program.

A *program* approach to English ministry is effective for at least two reasons. First, it provides multiple paths for demonstrating care for our students as whole people, not just as language learners. The enrichment or language practice activities in a program create many more opportunities for helping students with various life issues and developing friendships. Second, it provides more and diverse language-learning opportunities, increasing student potential for learning English well. Though we may like to think of ourselves as capable of leading our students to great heights of language acquisition in our English classes, the fact is that work done by the student outside of class often accounts for a great deal of their language learning. So by teaching students that all language learning does not happen in a typical language classroom and by providing them with varied opportunities for language learning outside an actual English class, we create more successful learners and a richer context for language learning.

What might such a program look like? Table 1 shows the kinds of activities that we used in the Brazilian English program, which was later also used in Indonesia. On the left are the opportunities for learning, followed by a description of the content and the suggested weekly timeframe. In order to better understand these activities, we will take a look at what the life of a typical student, Rosa, might look like in this program.

OPPORTUNITY FOR LEARNING	CONTENT	SUGGESTED HOURS PER WEEK
Core class (Levels 1–5)	The *English for Life* curriculum (overview in Appendix A) Supplementary grammar (using a grammar text) Bible verses (if appropriate)	4
Modules	High interest topics such as: Western cooking, effective parenting, crafts, health and fitness, movies, sports . . . whatever students are interested in! An opportunity to *use* English in a nonclassroom setting	1 per module (Students may be involved in several modules)
Group active learning	A class in which students of all levels learn together through singing, games, and other fun activities. Multilevel teaching techniques are used, and students are encouraged to help and support one another.	1
Self-directed learning	An opportunity for students to engage in individualized study utilizing the school's website	1
Conversation time (Either one-on-one or in small groups)	An opportunity for students to informally engage in conversation with a competent English speaker (who may not be a teacher)	15–20 minutes
Email buddies	An opportunity for students to have a pen pal overseas who will write to them in English (a good opportunity for volunteers in churches back home)	No specific time
Church services and other special events in English	These opportunities can significantly increase students' motivation in language learning and their exposure to English.	Monthly

Table 4. Program components

ROSA'S STORY

Rosa is a psychologist who works as a self-employed counselor. She is a nominal Catholic, is married and has two children in elementary school. She wants to learn English so she can attend conferences and access internet information in her field. Also, her family is saving up for a trip to Disney World, and she really wants to be able to communicate in English when she goes to the US. Rosa is in Level 2 in the English program. She has her Core Class on Monday and Wednesday mornings from 8:00–10:00. Her teacher is Brazilian. At first Rosa thought she needed to have a native English speaker as a teacher, but she soon discovered that her teacher is very good and can explain some of the grammar in Portuguese, which Rosa finds very helpful.

Right after her Core Class on Mondays she attends a Module on American cooking, which she loves. This teacher is American. Rosa's family really likes the American desserts she's learning to make! On Wednesdays after her Core Class she meets for fifteen minutes with her conversation partner—a Swiss woman who is in Brazil doing some short-term missions work with a local orphanage and who volunteers her time at the English school in exchange for Portuguese classes given by the Brazilian English teachers. Rosa usually brings a topic of conversation from her Core Class when she meets with her conversation partner. On Friday mornings there is "Song and Game Time" at the school. All of the levels are together, and it is really fun. They learn fun songs and play board games in which they practice English. Rosa has only attended twice because she has been too busy, but she would like to go more often.

On Saturdays Rosa works on her homework, part of which is to access the school's website and work on her independent learning project. She also tries to make time to write to her email buddy, Susan, who is a pastor's wife in Canada. Susan has never been to Brazil, and at first Rosa was very worried that her English would not be good enough to write to someone in Canada. But after a few emails she felt more at ease and now always looks forward to getting an email from her friend. Susan has even asked for Rosa's advice on counseling issues, because sometimes she counsels people at her church. It made Rosa feel good that she could give advice to someone in Canada—in English!

Rosa attended the English school's Fourth of July celebration with her family and really enjoyed it. Her kids especially loved roasting hot dogs and marshmallows! She has been invited to come to the school's monthly church service in English, but is not ready to do that yet. She doesn't know what to expect in a Protestant church and is afraid that she won't know enough English. But her husband has agreed that maybe they could go to the upcoming Christmas service. Rosa often tells her friends that this new English school she has found is really different. "They do a lot more than just grammar," she says. "I really enjoy being there, and I'm learning English too!"

It takes a lot of people to run a program with all of these different components. Our staff in Brazil consisted of fifteen full- and part-time teachers, half of whom were trained Brazilian English teachers and half of whom were short-term missionaries. It was an ideal environment for the learning and growth of all, including the teachers. But we did not begin with all these features. We started with Core Classes and then added the other components as we had personnel. A Christian program such as this one can have a significant positive impact on individuals and the community. When focused on providing a quality English-learning experience and meeting other student felt needs, it can be an effective vehicle for showing Christ's love.

As we now move on to the other English-ministry models, note that each of the formats below are represented, in some form, in the program described above. So if you have gotten excited about the potential of a full English program, read on for some ideas about developing the various components of such a program. In the following discussions it is important to bear in mind that the suggestions below are intended to provide some initial direction to those who may be new at teaching or at English ministries. They are *not* intended to replace a program of study designed to fully prepare an individual for English teaching.

COURSES

If ongoing English ministry is not a full-fledged program, it is likely a course. I use the term "course" here to talk about teaching a group of students which meets for several weeks or months to learn one specific subject. Sometimes the word "class" is used for this concept. A course could go by other names as well, such as "club" or "module." In Brazil we had a "Young Leader's Club" for adolescent English learners. This club met once a week, as a course, but in addition to the meeting times the students had service learning projects within the English school to fulfill throughout the week.

A course may operate as one of many within an institution, such as a course in a university. Or, it may be offered by an individual in an informal setting, such as a home Bible study. It may be in any of the four ministry types from

Chapter 3, and as such the topic may be grammar, English conversation, a book study, cooking, or study skills, just to name a few possibilities.

If we only see students once or twice a week for a few weeks or months, it can be hard to develop relationships that result in ministry. It is doubly essential, then, that such courses are run well. Though one can spend years acquiring all the knowledge necessary to teach well, I provide here some general guidelines to follow in many different teaching contexts.

TEN TIPS FOR ORGANIZING AND DELIVERING A COURSE

1. *Create the course schedule.*
   How often and how long will the course meet? Though all contexts are different, shorter courses of six to eight weeks are often more attractive to students than longer courses. Of course if you are teaching within a school, this course schedule is already set for you.
2. *Determine the course objectives—the learning goals.*
   What will students know or be able to do when they finish your course? Where English learning is concerned, it is best not to overstate course goals. "Students will be able to speak English fluently" is likely not an achievable goal in six weeks. However, "Students will read and discuss the biography of George Müller" would work in that time frame. Or "Students will gain practice in communicating about themselves, their families, and their communities" might be a good general objective statement for a low-level, semester-long general English course. (Learning goals are covered in more depth in Chapter 6.)
3. *Choose course materials.*
   In light of the course objectives, choose course materials that will enable students to meet the stated objectives. (This is addressed at length in Chapter 6.)
4. *Determine if formal assessment is needed throughout or at the end of the course.*
   If a grade is required, determine how you will assess learning. While you may immediately think "test" when considering assessment, there are often more effective ways to evaluate language skills. Students could use a task checklist (see, for example, the *English for Life* task checklists in Appendix A), develop portfolios demonstrating their work, or present a final speech, poster, booklet, or play to showcase their language skills.
5. *Create a topical syllabus.*
   Give the course objectives, materials, and assessment, and show what will be

studied or learned in each class session. An example of a topical syllabus can be found in Appendix B.

6. *Plan some regular features of each class.*
For example, you may want to open with a proverb or finish with an "exit question" (a question or set of questions over something learned, that must be answered by students as they leave the class). Familiar routines can help students feel comfortable in a class and also save the teacher from planning every class event anew for each class meeting.
7. *Create a lesson plan for each class.*
Most lesson plans include the following: a review of previous work, an introduction to new material, activities to practice new material, and preparation for homework. An example of a lesson plan can be found in Appendix C.
8. *Be enthusiastic, optimistic, and flexible in class.*
The teacher usually sets the class tone. A positive, low-stress environment is much more effective for language learning than a demanding, rigid one. Lesson plans never unfold exactly as envisioned during the planning stage, therefore flexibility (and a ready file of activities in case the class lasts longer than your lesson) is important. However, chaos is not helpful, so creating an environment in which there is respect among all is essential.
9. *Meet students' needs.*
The course is not about you, it's about them. You are not there to entertain them or dazzle them, but to enable them to learn. So pay attention to whether and how well students are learning. Listen and watch as they use newly acquired language in speech and writing. Can they actually use the language you are teaching them? Reteach and reinforce as needed to ensure learning. Don't rush through material just to get to the end. Reformulate your syllabus and sequencing if needed so that real learning can take place. Always endeavor to teach the real students in your class, not the ideal students that you wish them to be.
10. *Teach the individuals in your class, not the class as a group.*
Use their names when you speak to them, and respect their unique opinions and ideas. Tailor learning activities around their interests and learning styles as much as possible. Be in touch with them outside of class occasionally, if appropriate in your context. In many teaching situations you may be able to send short, encouraging emails or text messages a few times during the course. A phone call after an absence may be very much appreciated.

Such activities must be culturally appropriate, and of course must be ethical in both intent and appearance. (It is very important to ask local teachers how such contact may be perceived, and it is difficult to be too cautious where cross-gender communication is concerned.) But when used appropriately, such contact can make the teacher-student relationship a much more effective and personal one, both for language learning and for meeting other needs that students may have.

MIGUEL'S STORY

Miguel is in his third year in a business program in a university in Mexico City. He is required to take a class in English for Business, and this year the teacher is a man named Joe who happens to be studying Spanish in Mexico. (After Joe learns the language he will be moving to another part of Mexico to head up a micro-financing project that is run by a mission organization.) On the first day of class Miguel receives a course syllabus telling him what he will be studying and what text he will be using. He is a little surprised to discover that the students will be developing fictitious businesses and conducting simulated meetings in class. He will not just be memorizing material and taking a test on it. (Joe is using developmental teaching methods.)

As Miguel gets into the coursework he has trouble with one assignment—researching and evaluating the ethical track record of a business. (Joe is using edifying content as he asks students to investigate ethics in business.) After class one day Miguel stayed to ask the teacher a question about the assignment. He was then very surprised the next day when he received a text message from the teacher asking him how the assignment was going and if he needed more help. None of his teachers had ever done that before.

Every day his teacher shouts out a friendly, "Hi Miguel!" when he walks into class. Increasingly, they chat a little before class begins. Though Miguel has a very busy semester he never wants to miss his English class. He is contemplating asking the teacher if he would be willing to talk to him about how to get a job in a multinational business. He hopes that he will be able to keep in touch with this teacher when the course is over.

Miguel's story shows the impact that one teacher can have on one student (and possibly many more) during one course. Even if Joe only teaches this one English course before going on to his "real" ministry assignment, Miguel's life has been touched forever, and a lasting friendship may result.

TUTORING OR COACHING

While few missionaries may go to the field initially just to tutor or be a conversation partner, many who go with other job descriptions eventually end up taking on such roles occasionally. Perhaps they have a neighbor who constantly pleads with them for help with English. Or a national colleague wants to get together to practice his English conversation skills before receiving a delegation of international visitors. In fact, this kind of one-on-one language assistance can be one of the most productive in terms of ministry and can fall under any of the four ministry types in Chapter 3. Usually it is characterized by few governmental or institutional constraints, a friendship or the anticipation of a friendship, and a student who is willing, eager, and open.

I have spoken with missionaries who dread hearing a request with the word "tutor" in it. They have been turned off to tutoring because they feel it takes the same amount of preparation as a course, but with only one beneficiary. But there is another, less teacher-intensive way to look at tutoring. It has incredible potential for developing *learner autonomy*, a cutting-edge buzzword in TESOL today. Learner autonomy is the idea that students learn best when *they,* not the teacher, define what it is that they need and want to learn, and take the lead in their learning. In tutoring arrangements it can be the *student* who invests time and energy in developing a syllabus tailored to his or her needs, finding materials, and planning a course of study. Students as young as upper elementary[12] may be able to take a large hand in directing their tutoring sessions. In this type of tutoring the tutor's role is that of a *guide on the side*, or a *coach* in the task of language acquisition. When tutoring is characterized by work done primarily by the learner rather than by the teacher, it becomes less of a time burden for the tutor and a positive source of development and learning for the student. Such an arrangement is one of the best developmental teaching methods that exists, which we saw in Chapter 3 contributes to English ministry. And though the concept of student control over learning is a new one in some cultures, most students who request tutors will respond positively to it and meet the challenge.

Still it will usually fall to the tutor to set up the tutoring arrangement at the beginning and coach the student into the role of taking more responsibility for

12 When working with children it is very important to involve the parents in planning the tutoring arrangement and to keep them informed throughout the duration of the tutoring agreement.

his or her learning. So I provide here some guidelines for getting started in this type of tutoring arrangement:

TEN TIPS FOR GETTING STARTED WITH LEARNER-CONTROLLED TUTORING

1. At the initial meeting, *before you commit to the tutoring arrangement,* find out the student's:
    a. Learning goals. Some students have not thought much about their goals, and may need to get back to you after a day or two of pondering what they really want to learn.
    b. Time commitment. How often does the student want to meet? For how long?
    c. Preferred learning activities. What does the student envision doing during tutoring sessions?
2. Take some time to think through the student's answers to the above questions, considering whether or not you can be of help to the student. Even though an individual may plead for help, it is best not to enter into an arrangement unless you feel you are truly able to help the student meet his specific learning goals.
3. Share with the student the concept of learner control. Explain that the best learning is that in which the student does most of the work. Together come to an agreement on the intended teacher-student roles in the tutoring arrangement. Such an agreement might be as simple as "You will bring the learning activities for each session, and I will answer your questions as you do them."
4. Define the location, frequency, and duration of the meeting times; establish approximate beginning and ending dates. While it may feel awkward to begin informal tutoring by setting an ending date, in the long run it seems that most people do best with a defined and limited period for the tutoring arrangement. *At this point, establish the tutoring agreement.* In some cultures it may be appropriate to have an informal contract defining the arrangement, particularly if any kind of payment is involved. In other contexts the agreement may be a friendly and informal one, and making it overly formal could imply lack of trust.
5. Even if the student has agreed to plan the tutoring sessions, the tutor may need to initiate some of the learning activities or provide suggestions until

the student begins to understand the types of things that may help him learn. What learning activities may be suitable depends on the topic, age of the student, and learning goals.

6. Begin each tutoring session connecting with the student. Take a personal interest by asking what has been happening in the student's life. Share some about your own life as well. This is relationship-building time. Don't shy away from sharing your faith or even praying with the student if the context is appropriate for this. Consider the *student* first and foremost when contemplating such actions. Never do or say anything that would make the student uncomfortable or put him at risk in any way.
7. During the tutoring session let the student direct his learning. This is a new concept for many students, and they may need occasional prompts such as, "How can I help you in your learning today?" or "What kind of activity might work well for you to practice using this new information?"
8. Look for opportunities to encourage the use of edifying content. For example, if the student suggests writing a letter as a learning activity, you could extend this thought by suggesting that the student write a letter putting forward a way to address the problem of poverty in his city.
9. At the end of each session, initiate an informal evaluation of how the session went. Some possible questions include: "In what ways did today's session help you?" and "Is there anything you would like to do differently at our next session?" This is a good time to encourage the student to plan for the next session, by asking a question such as "What are you going to prepare this coming week for our next tutoring session?"
10. Close each session with affirmation. It is especially beneficial to affirm the student's developing learner autonomy. Comment on initiative that the student has taken to develop his own language skills. Even if the student has not shown stellar capacity to plan his own learning experience, compliment him on whatever he has done that was useful, such as taking notes or bringing in reading material. Show genuine anticipation for the next meeting time. Be warm, enthusiastic, and positive.

MUSA'S STORY

Musa is an ambitious Malaysian sixteen year old. Though his parents are relatively uneducated and he attends a poor public high school, he really wants to learn English, go to college, and make something of himself. He has already picked up a lot of

English from movies and music, but he feels he needs help in order to really do well on the English portion of the national exam.

An older woman from New Zealand lives a couple of houses down from him. During one community event she made some cookies and shared them with all the neighbors. Musa talked with her a little that day, and she said he reminded her of her grandson back in New Zealand. So when Musa needed help preparing for the English portion of the national exam he thought maybe she could help him. One day he saw her outside and he got up the courage to ask, and soon they were having tea on the front porch talking about the help he needed.

Musa was very nervous at first, but he soon discovered that Mrs. Austin was kind and easy to talk to. She spoke Malay well, and so he could communicate easily with her. She asked him what he wanted help with, and he explained that he wanted to do well on the national exam. She asked him what kinds of questions were on the exam, and he wasn't sure. He was a little surprised when she said that she would be happy to help him, but she wanted him to come prepared each session with what to study. He took up the challenge and got a practice test from his teacher to use during their sessions.

After a few meeting times on Mrs. Austin's porch, he felt very comfortable talking to her. They often talked about their families. Mrs. Austin would share about her grandson in New Zealand and Musa would tell about his life and ambitions as he practiced verb tenses and prepositions. Musa soon felt freedom to express that he wanted to be different from his family. Mrs. Austin always encouraged him to respect his parents and talk with them about his dreams. At each closing session, she told him that God loved him and had made him for a special purpose. Musa had always thought of God as stern, not as someone who loved him. This gave him a lot to think about.

Mrs. Austin is probably having more of an impact on Musa's life than she realizes. She is helping him to prepare for the national exam, which may expand his future choices in life. She is also affirming and supporting his family and culture, while still gently helping him to see and feel God's love. His life may be vastly different than it would have been without tea and English on Mrs. Austin's porch.

SPECIAL EVENTS

We have looked at English-learning formats from the macro to the micro, from large school programs to one-on-one tutoring. Now we turn our attention to the last of the four formats: special events. Events for English learners can be those which actively seek to teach English, those which provide a context for practicing English, or those which seek to build bridges and cultural understanding. A special event could take place in an evening, a day, or a week. English camps are a type of special event, as are parties, presentations, and even religious services. A special event would most likely be of the *host* type, and possibly more often oriented towards evangelism than discipleship.

Events are often possible because of visiting English speakers coming to the field on mission trips. Mission trips have become so common for North Americans that it is now fairly unusual to find an active church member who has never been on one, and according to Livermore (2006), a great deal of the increase in participation in mission trips has come in the teen population. Much has been written about the potential dangers of such trips, from the skewed emphasis on the participant over the good of those receiving services, to the burden on career missionaries and nationals who are repeatedly receiving foreign groups. Livermore and others (e.g., Priest, 2008) have provided insightful commentary on the pros and cons of short-term missions, and I refer readers to those resources rather than delve into the discussion here.

The reality for English ministry, though, is that mission trips do occur with increasing frequency, and as missionaries on the field, it behooves us to seek ways to help them be a blessing rather than an annoyance. One of these ways is through English-medium events, aimed at meeting the needs of English-language learners. When I worked in Brazil I remember an enthusiastic American youth leader wanting to bring a group of teens to Brazil to evangelize by passing out tracts in the town square. These teens would not have been able to engage in any conversation with the recipients of the tracts, because they did not speak Portuguese. Such feel-good evangelism (evangelism that makes the *evangelist* feel good) would be unlikely to bear any real fruit and might have actually turned off Brazilians who would pass by and feel patronized by this approach. These teens, instead, were offered the opportunity to come and work alongside Brazilian teens who were learning English, to organize a special event for our school. This would enable them to be cultural learners and provide an actual service in conversing with the Brazilian teens in English.

Special events can vary a great deal in format and purpose, from weeklong English camps to one-evening parties. It may be presumptuous to try to conceive of a list of tips or best practice for such diverse events, but I will endeavor to do so here.

TEN TIPS FOR CONDUCTING EVENTS

1. *Use a cross-cultural team approach when envisioning and planning events.*
   For example, if the event is an English camp in Korea, with a goal of helping participants to improve their English and learn about American culture, it would be ideal to have both American and Korean English teachers on the planning committee.
2. *Define the English- and/or culture-learning goal(s).*
   Remember that the first part of English ministry is *English.* While culture learning and building friendships are also legitimate aspects of language learning, first and foremost participants usually want to develop skill in using English.
3. *Define the ministry goal.*
   Remember that *ministry* is also a part of English ministry. In our program in Brazil, special events not only provided extra English learning for our students, but they also were a drawing card for students contemplating entering our program. In other cases, special events might be overtly evangelistic, such as in the showing of a Christian film, or oriented towards discipleship, such as hosting a special low-English-level seminar for seminary students.
4. *Be transparent in goals and marketing.*
   If the purpose of the event is for potential students to get to know an English program or course, that goal should be made clear. If religious content will be used, those who attend should not be surprised by that. The English camp story in Chapter 3 illustrates the need for transparency in marketing.
5. *Organize well.*
   It takes a great deal of planning and organization to pull off a larger event such as an English camp well (see Appendix D for suggestions). We usually began planning our English camps in Brazil six months beforehand. Even events of a few hours often require weeks of planning. Part of the testimony in English ministry comes from quality. Quality events are the result of planning. It is best not to underestimate the number of people that will be needed or the amount of time it will take to plan.

6. *Spread the jobs around.*
   It can often be a great learning experience for English students to participate in leadership in special events. I have found that using more people for smaller jobs often results in the greatest amount of learning through the event. People who plan events can tend to be do-it-yourself types who run around out of breath during the event, not enjoying it at all, simply because they didn't invite enough participation. I know because I am one of these types by nature!
7. *Clearly define roles.*
   For example, if someone is designated as a greeter for an event, what does that mean? Where is she supposed to stand? How long should she stay at her post? Define these roles in advance.
8. *Register participants in some way.*
   Perhaps they will register for a drawing for free books or lessons. Have a box for them to check on the registration form if they do *not* want to receive information about future events or classes, and respect their wishes not to be contacted. You will have contact information for those who do not check this box.
9. *Be flexible.*
   This is especially important for Westerners to remember when involved in events in more process-oriented cultures. Though we may wow the local culture with our impressive minute-by-minute organization and efficiency, we should also show humility and deference if people do things that mess up our schedules. People are more important than schedules. Our cross-cultural team approach to running events in Brazil helped me learn this. When things did not go according to plan, it was the Brazilian teachers who could adapt, modify, show flexibility, and ensure that everyone had a good time despite the glitches. I learned a great deal from them.
10. *Evaluate.*
    If the event is a larger one such as a camp, a seminar, or a workshop, have an evaluation form for participants to fill out. For all events, regardless of duration, meet with the staff following the event to evaluate its effectiveness. Thank the staff and accept any words of advice that they have to offer. Write up a report on the event, and make sure the report can be easily accessed prior to the next event.

SOFIA'S STORY

Sofia is a shy third-grader in an elementary school in Indonesia. Her English teacher is from America and in the last English class she said that there would be an "English Day" next week. The teacher said there would be lots of fun things to do and American food. Sofia doesn't know what to expect and is a little nervous about it.

On English Day, Sofia is surprised when she comes to school. There are ten foreigners there! They are all big and tall and white. She is a little scared until she sees her teacher, who smiles at her and shows her where to go. During the morning there are no normal classes. Instead, Sofia goes from room to room with her classmates, and there are foreigners teaching different things in each room. In one room she learns about a place called Canada. She gets to taste some sweet syrup and gets a red-and-white pencil. In another room there are musical instruments called recorders. She discovers that she can play a song! She doesn't want to leave this room. In another room she makes a little booklet telling about herself, and the foreigners even take a picture of her that comes out instantly, which she pastes in her booklet.

Finally, she goes with her classmates out to the courtyard. At first she doesn't understand what is happening. The foreigners give her a plastic bag, then put cream and sugar into it. Sofia has never seen cream before. It looks yucky. Then at another table they help her put her little bag into a bigger bag with ice and salt in it. She thinks the foreigners are crazy when they tell her to shake it for ten minutes and the cream will become ice cream. She and her classmates have fun shaking and throwing their bags. Finally, she takes her bag to her teacher and asks if she is done. Her teacher opens her bag and gives her a spoon . . . it really is ice cream! Sofia can hardly believe her eyes.

Sofia goes home after school that day and tells her mom about all the interesting things she did. She knows she will NEVER forget this day!

Sofia experienced the "English Day" that I organized with help from a wonderful short-term group from the US and Canada, for the elementary school where I taught. The goal of this event was primarily culture learning and building relationships at the school, though some English learning took place as well. My prayer is that Sofia will remember the kindness, happiness, and caring of all the foreigners who came to her school that day, and that this experience will, in the long run, result in a better understanding of Westerners and Christians than she might have had otherwise.

CONCLUSION

English ministry can be large or small. It can be the main ministry assignment of several people and can provide jobs for local Christian English teachers when it is a full program. Or it can be one person donating a few hours of time to help a neighbor down the street. It can involve short-termers who come just for a week for special events, or those who come to stay a little longer, teaching a class for a semester. Whatever the size and shape that English ministry takes, it can serve to meet English-learning needs and open pathways for life-changing relationships to be built.

DISCUSSION AND APPLICATION

1. Look at Rosa's story. Make a list of all the factors contributing to her English learning. Now make a list of the ways that *ministry* is taking place in her story (you may want to refer back to Chapter 3).
2. Look at the "Ten Tips for Organizing and Delivering a Course." Which three of these do you think are most often neglected in English ministries, and why?
3. Imagine that you are teacher "Joe" in Miguel's story, and that you are asked, after the course is finished, about the ministry impact of that teaching assignment. How would you justify the teaching of this Business English class as ministry to your superiors?
4. Have you ever experienced learner-controlled tutoring either as a learner or as a teacher? If so, describe that experience. If not, describe what you see as the benefits and drawbacks for both learner and teacher in this type of tutoring arrangement.
5. Look at Musa's story. Describe how Mrs. Austin has ministered to Musa, while still displaying cultural sensitivity and respect.
6. Look at the "Ten Tips for Conducting Events." Think of a particular context in which a group of Westerners on a mission trip might participate in an English event overseas. For this particular context, which three of the ten tips do you think might be most important, and why?
7. Look at Sofia's story. How might her life be impacted by English Day? How might that event change the foreign participants? Would the impact of this event be lessened if there were not regular, long-term English ministry happening at the school?

CHAPTER 6

ENGLISH CLASSES: THREE BUILDING BLOCKS

We have looked at types of ministry, teacher preparation, and various formats of English instruction. Now we want to look closely at an English class. We will ask: What ingredients are necessary to foster effective language learning in a classroom environment, and how can these be ministry oriented? The three areas that we will look at are *curriculum, methodology,* and *materials*—the building blocks of classroom learning.

There are excellent courses and books which can and should be used to help teachers understand what transpires in an effective classroom. There is a lot to consider that is not addressed in this book. Classroom management, for instance, is a very important topic in teacher preparation. There is a great deal to know about how to handle different age groups, different size classes, and different language levels. Teaching the different skill areas (reading, writing, speaking, and listening) is also not addressed here. So while this book (and especially this chapter) may seem to the TESOL novice to provide a lot of information about teaching, it by no means provides a comprehensive understanding of classroom teaching.

Don Snow has written two excellent books for beginning English teachers. *More Than a Native Speaker: An Introduction to Teaching English Abroad* (2006), oriented towards native English speakers, and *From Language Learner to Language Teacher: An Introduction to Teaching English as a Foreign Language* (2007), oriented towards nonnative English speakers. Books such as these can provide the understanding that beginning teachers need. In addition, at least a short certificate course in TESOL is recommended for most involved in English ministry (recall the discussion in Chapter 4 on training needs). This chapter is not meant to provide a comprehensive understanding of curriculum, methodology, and materials, but rather to discuss their role and use in English ministry.

THE HEART OF CLASSROOM CHOICES

One question lies at the heart of all decisions regarding curriculum, methods, and materials: *What are the goals?* Unless we define our goals well, we have no basis on which to select appropriate classroom content and strategies. In English ministries, we have two essential goals to define:

1. What are the English-learning goals?
2. What are the ministry goals?

Only when we have defined these goals can we move forward. Therefore, we will look briefly here at what goals may look like before moving on to our discussions of curriculum, methods, and materials. We have touched on goals elsewhere in this book, as when we looked at learning goals in relation to teacher preparation in Chapter 4, or in relation to models for English ministry in Chapter 5. Some of the discussion in this chapter will overlap with what has been said earlier. But here we want to look specifically at goals as they pertain to how we organize and deliver English classes.

English-learning goals may be very broad, for example, "To develop English to an advanced level." Presumably learners with this goal want to develop all four skill areas (listening, speaking, reading, and writing) to a level suitable for university study or professional work. Such a goal would be suitable for a complete program, not an individual course. A low-intermediate course-level goal might be "To be able to communicate orally with foreign visitors about my family and my job." At the lesson level for a beginner's class, we might find the goal "To be able to talk about a past event using the verbs *have, make,* and *do* in their past-tense forms." Such a goal for an individual lesson is often called a *learning objective.*

Though it is not always easy to define English-learning goals accurately, it can be considerably more difficult to nail down ministry goals. Part of the difficulty lies in the fact that we often may not know what kind of ministry will be possible before we get into the job. As suggested in Chapter 3, ministry may be defined more in terms of a sequence of possibilities rather than a definite plan. Still, without some kind of ministry goal as we go into English ministry, we may be in danger of living out that old axiom, "If you shoot at nothing you will hit it every time." Instead, I suggest that it is appropriate to define ministry goals at the outset, while maintaining the flexibility to change them as needed.

Like English-learning goals, ministry goals may vary from the very broad to the more specific. A very broad goal such as, "Get to know a few students personally" may have little to do with the classroom planning issues that are the topic of this chapter. But other ministry goals will indeed impact lesson planning. Consider, for instance, the goal "To develop students' ability to think critically." This necessitates the selection of methodologies that will develop critical thought processes. Or a more specific ministry goal may determine material selection, such as, "To replace the textbook reading on actress Pamela Anderson, showcasing her work on animal rights, with a text on actor Kirk Cameron, showcasing his work promoting strong marital values in film."

At the beginning of any of the four English-ministry models outlined in Chapter 5 (program, course, tutoring, or event) it is crucial that we outline the English-learning and ministry goals that we hope to reach through whatever it is that we are offering. Once we have defined these goals, we can begin our planning. We need to plan the *curriculum:* what will be learned; the *methodology:* how the learning will take place; and the *materials:* what resources will aid the learning. These three aspects of planning are necessary in most English-ministry contexts. The only exception is when actual teaching is not being done, as in some of the event scenarios mentioned in Chapter 5, or when the English ministry is a tutoring arrangement which is being led by the student. Even in such cases, the concepts described below should be considered and adapted however they may apply to the ministry context.

CURRICULUM

Though the word *curriculum* can be used in numerous ways, I use it in this chapter as an overall plan of study to achieve a specific goal. If the goal is English fluency in speaking, listening, reading, and writing, a curriculum might contain topics progressing from the very basic learning of letters and numbers, to communication about oneself, to the development of advanced reading and writing skills (as does the *English for Life* curriculum in Appendix A). Or it may be organized in terms of skills or functions such as "listening for general ideas" or "making requests."

An English-learning context might not have general English learning as a goal, but rather one specific area of language development, such as academic writing. A curriculum might then be a semester-long plan outlining learning tasks to help students develop academic writing skills. Such a plan for a single course is often called a *syllabus.*

Often a textbook or a textbook series is adopted, and its curriculum becomes the curriculum for the course. Sometimes a certain textbook is required by the institution. In addition, this may be the only way to organize a course of study when teachers are untrained and those making decisions about the course or program do not have a background in TESOL or even in education. Unfortunately, this has often been the case in English-ministry endeavors. However, there are dangers in simply allowing the textbook to be the curriculum. First, it ties one to the textbook, and thus to the drawbacks of textbook use, which are outlined below in the section on materials.

Second, this approach often results in teachers not taking sufficient ownership of the course. When each class session is approached the night before (or five minutes before!) with the attitude of "Let's see what we're doing next in the textbook," then the textbook is leading the course, not the teacher. Teachers who approach English teaching in this way often do not have a clear picture of the overall goals of the course, and though the curriculum may be laid out in the front of the book, they likely have not studied it or thought to modify it to better fit their students' needs.

For these reasons, I believe that in *all* English-ministry contexts it is a good idea to have a curriculum (or a syllabus) to direct learning. Furthermore, the teacher needs to be very familiar with the curriculum, preferably taking a hand in developing the portions of it that he or she will be teaching.

TEN TIPS FOR PLANNING CURRICULA FOR ENGLISH MINISTRIES

1. *Write broad English-learning goals.*

   These may be goals that extend beyond your own part in the learning process. Look at the big picture of the students' language-learning experiences. If students are in university, for instance, what does their whole English-learning program look like? Or, if you are tutoring a student for a specific course, what is the goal of that course?

   Example: "Students in this program want to develop intermediate speaking and listening skills, and advanced reading skills."

   Though we may feel that we do not need to concern ourselves with the parts of student learning in which we are not directly involved, I believe that this is a mistake. We need to care about, and show that we care about, students' long-term goals. We need to understand where they have come from and where they are going in order to meet their current needs effectively.

2. *Write specific English-learning goals.*
   Find out where your piece fits into the big picture. Are you teaching one course within a larger language-learning system? What will students need to learn in your course so they will be adequately prepared for the next step?
   Example: "Students in my reading class want to develop the ability to read intermediate-level texts, understanding the main ideas and key vocabulary."
3. *Write English-ministry goals.*
   Which of the four types of English ministry highlighted in Chapter 3 is this English-teaching assignment? Consider what you know of the context, culture, and students. Define broad ministry goals as best you can with the knowledge that you have before the class begins and you meet the students.
   Examples: "I will pray for my students every day" or "I will use some edifying texts" or "I will use some developmental teaching methods."
   A ministry goal should never detract from or negate an English-learning goal. This would mean that we value our own agenda over that of our students. As ministry goals are determined, they should *enhance* English learning, never hinder it. Good ministry goals will always also be good for students' English learning.
4. *Create an initial curriculum guide outlining what students will study.*
   If this is for an individual course and also includes a week-by-week outline of what will be studied, it might be called a syllabus. It is important to do this even if you are using a textbook and it seems as though you are simply copying the table of contents as you prepare your curriculum. You may be surprised at how much you will modify as you engage in this task of creating your own curriculum. (See Appendix B for a sample course syllabus that meets specific English and ministry goals.)
5. *Consider your teaching methods (see the discussion on methodology below).*
   Ensure that your curriculum is compatible with the methods you want to use. For example, if you are assigned to teach intermediate reading, you may be given as a possible text one which utilizes isolated paragraphs that students read, looking for main ideas and topic sentences. You may feel, however, that reading is better developed by having the class read through a novel during the course, and having students demonstrate their understanding through

debates, discussion groups, and response journals related to the content of the novel. Such a switch from a skill-focused approach to a meaning-focused approach to reading would result in considerable change to the curriculum.

6. *Select your materials (see the discussion on materials below).*
   Ensure that the materials you use will truly meet the students' learning goals. Often it is necessary at this point to alter the curriculum a bit in order to accommodate the materials that you have decided to use. For example, perhaps you have found a text that covers the topics you have selected, only in a different order. You will then want to align your curriculum with the specific text that you have chosen to use.
7. *Consider other learning opportunities (showcased under "programs" in Chapter 5).*
   Even at the level of curriculum planning, consider how you will encourage students to become autonomous learners, developing language skills on their own, outside of the classroom. This may be reflected, for instance, in the inclusion of individual or group learning projects as part of the curriculum, or in making correspondence with email buddies a course requirement.
8. *If the students are teens or older, give them a copy of the curriculum at the beginning of the course.*
   If there is a larger curriculum and your course is only a part of it, spend some time talking about the big picture of students' learning and the role that your course plays in it. Too often we don't help students to see their learning holistically and to understand how various components of their studies fit together. Then go over your own curriculum, ensuring that students get a general idea of what they will be learning in your class.
9. *Modify the curriculum if needed as the course progresses, providing students with the modified curriculum.*
   If you have taught a course several times you may not need any modifications throughout the course. But if our classes are truly responsive to students' needs and interests, as we want them to be, this usually means that we will need to make some modifications to our original plan as we teach the course. Any modifications should be made in order to better meet the original English-learning and ministry goals.
10. *After the course is finished, evaluate the curriculum.*
    Here are some questions to ask:
    - Did the course meet the English-learning goals?
    - Did you meet the ministry goals?

- Did the text or other chosen materials work well and contribute to meeting the goals?
- Did the students feel that the course was effective? Are there any changes that they have suggested? (A course evaluation completed by the students is important to provide this information.)

Compile this information and decide what changes you would make the next time you or someone else teaches this course.

METHODOLOGY

Just as there are many different meanings of "curriculum," there are a variety of uses of the word "methodology." Sometimes it is used to refer to very specific techniques or processes used by a teacher in a classroom. Other times it is much more general, denoting all the activities in a classroom which are meant to foster learning. My use of the term here is in this broader sense. I will not be speaking of "methods" per se. A TESOL course or a study of TESOL texts is recommended to learn a variety of methods, techniques, and activities for teaching English. In this discussion, I will relate the choice of methodology specifically to ministry goals.

BEYOND METHODS

First, however, I do want to address a relevant shift in the field of TESOL. In the latter part of the twentieth century many new language-teaching methods were developed, as researchers and teachers searched for the perfect way to learn and teach a language. The culmination of this pursuit of methods was in *Communicative Language Teaching (CLT),* which currently remains the latest and probably most well-known "method" (though CLT would more correctly be called an "approach") for teaching English. CLT emphasizes the learning of language through real communication as opposed to memorization and drills.

According to Kumaravadivelu (2006) and others, we are now in the era of postmethods. That is, language teaching is not considered to be primarily about methodology, but about how we understand language learning and teaching. Brown (2001) addresses this shift by providing a list of *principles* for language learning. Among his principles are such notions as the importance of motivation and self-image in successful language learning and the idea that culture learning should go hand in hand with language learning. Brown's twelve principles are provided in Appendix G, as they can help both novice and experienced teachers understand language acquisition.

Kumaravadivelu's (2006) alternative to methods takes the form of *strategies*. These are fundamental teaching concepts that he believes should guide teacher actions. Though some of these are more readily understandable to those new to TESOL than others, I provide them here in order to convey the general idea of what is meant by teaching strategies.

Kumaravadivelu's (2006, p. 201) macro-strategies for teaching English:

1. Maximize learning opportunities.
2. Facilitate negotiated interaction.
3. Minimize perceptual mismatches.
4. Activate intuitive heuristics (problem-solving by trial and error).
5. Foster language awareness.
6. Contextualize linguistic input.
7. Integrate language skills (reading, writing, speaking, and listening).
8. Promote learner autonomy.
9. Ensure social relevance.
10. Raise cultural consciousness.

Both Brown's principles and Kumaravadivelu's strategies deal with the underlying goals of language learning and teaching rather than with specific methods or approaches used to reach those goals. For example, a teacher needs to understand the principle that "students learn through practice" and the strategy of "maximizing learning opportunities." A teacher who has internalized these principles and strategies will make choices in the classroom that result in student learning. This may involve methods and techniques such as asking more questions, using more pair and group work, and providing more wait time for student responses. Student learning is achieved not primarily because certain methods or techniques are being used, but because the teaching is based on certain principles and guided by effective strategies.

DEVELOPMENTAL TEACHING METHODS

In several of the preceding chapters in this book I have referred to *developmental teaching methods*. I use this phrase to describe methodology which does not simply result in the acquisition of information or facts, but goes one step further to *develop the person*. To illustrate this concept, think of a child in a third-grade

English class in Indonesia. This student is learning words related to the kitchen. One approach to teaching this class might be to show students pictures of the items in a kitchen and have them memorize the English words for these items. A test would probably be given on these words, then the teacher would move on.

This approach results in learning the words, but does not develop the child in any other way. Imagine, however, that learning these words is followed by a simple story about a brother and sister helping their mother in the kitchen. Included in the story is thankfulness for both food and family. This English lesson has not stopped with the learning of new words, but has hopefully helped to develop notions of helpfulness and thankfulness in the students. Taking this idea further, let's suppose the story left out a few words, which children had to guess at. As they work in pairs to fill in the missing words, critical thought processes are being developed. Finally, imagine that the homework was to help do something in the kitchen, then share the next day how you helped. Now we have taken the theory of helpfulness and put it into action. Such a lesson sequence can develop far more than English! But all of these activities are helpful for learning English as well. This is what I call developmental teaching.

Developmental teaching methods will vary greatly with different age groups and different contexts. Here I provide a very limited list of activities which can be used with many different age groups and English levels.

Ten Ways to Teach Developmentally

1. *Teach constructively.*

   "Constructivism" means choosing classroom activities in which students *discover* or *construct* meaning, rather than those in which they are *given* information. (See Brooks and Brooks, 1993, for a short, easy-to-read guide to constructivist teaching.) It is teaching inductively rather than deductively. Though constructivism is not appropriate for all teaching contexts and content areas, when appropriate it can help students develop critical thinking and take ownership of their learning.

   Example: Instead of explaining how to add "-ed" to make past tense in English and then having students practice by filling in blanks in random sentences, show students a list of sentences talking about the past. Have them discover the rule and then apply it by talking about their own past activities.

2. *Use projects.*

   Project based learning (PBL) has moved to the forefront in language teaching, and in education as a whole. As students work on projects together to discover and apply information, they take ownership of what they are learning and are able to use language for real communication purposes.

Example: As students are learning words related to emotions, have them work in groups to create booklets with photographs of themselves expressing certain emotions. Since facial expressions can be cultural, their booklets can serve as a guide for foreigners new to the country. (See the project component of the *English for Life* curriculum in Appendix A for more examples.)

3. *Ask more than you tell.*
   Never tell students what they can tell you! Ask higher order questions which require students to analyze, synthesize, and evaluate. (See Bloom's Taxonomy for a list of higher-order thinking functions.) Remember the story in Chapter 3 of the school in Asia where the children did not understand that they were being asked a question and could only respond with rote repetition? Sometimes simply teaching students to answer information questions can be helpful in developing critical thought processes.

   Example: To teach university students about the features of business correspondence, a "telling" teacher might hand out copies of a business letter and then lecture about its features. An "asking" teacher, on the other hand, would ask the students to identify the features that make the letter businesslike, listing them on the board as students offer suggestions.
4. *Use individualized learning plans.*
   We have previously discussed the value of learner autonomy—a student's sense of responsibility for and ability to engage in their own learning. Having all students create learning plans and providing one-on-one conferencing as they achieve their learning goals results in both increased learner autonomy and a more personal teacher-student relationship.

   Example: A teacher discovers that her students vary greatly in their writing abilities. She asks them to each set their own writing tasks for the semester, from creating a short paragraph telling about themselves to writing a several-page paper on a topic of interest. She meets with students individually to help them through multiple drafts and to dialogue with them about their topics.
5. *Activate different learning styles.*
   In many parts of the world, education is geared to those who excel at reading, writing, and memorizing. English class can provide much-needed

opportunities for those who need experiential learning, or who learn best by processing information verbally in a small group.

Example: A traditional class may require high school students to memorize verb tenses. An experientially based class might instead have students work in groups to create and present a play that uses the verb tenses to be learned.

6. *Use appropriate teacher talk.*
Students learn when they can understand, not when they can't. Teachers sometimes do not gear their own language to the level of the students. Speaking too quickly and using too many extraneous words are common problems. Stephen Krashen (1981) has labeled a student's optimal language-learning level as i+1—one level higher than the student's current (independent) language level. We will see later the importance of this concept in relation to the selection of materials, but here the point is that the talk of the classroom must also be at the i+1 level, neither too difficult nor too easy. When students can follow what is being said even though it is a stretch for them, the conditions are ideal for developing their skills in not only language but also in thinking and reasoning.

Example: A teacher of low-intermediate junior high students commonly makes statements like this: "Okay everybody why don't you all get out your books right now and I think we left off yesterday at page thirty-nine, was that right?" Especially if spoken quickly, much of this may be unintelligible at this level. Instead, the teacher could say slowly and clearly, "Please take out your books and turn to page thirty-nine."

7. *Use music and games.*[13]
Using music provides instant motivation for many students. When students listen for words in a song, contemplate underlying messages in songs, or work with a group to write and sing songs, they are engaged in many different types of developmental activities. Games can provide similar opportunities. Games can involve analysis, application, evaluation, and other higher-order thinking skills. And . . . students love them!

Example: A teacher has taught words for body parts and now wishes to review. She asks students to come to the board one at a time and write the word as she points to a part of her body. After twenty-five words have been written, she

---

13 There are many teacher resource books providing songs and games for the English classroom. A simple internet search will yield many possibilities.

hands out blank Bingo sheets with twenty-five squares. She instructs the students to randomly write the words on the board in the squares on their Bingo sheets. She then plays Bingo by pointing to a part of her body (not saying the word), and having students draw an X over the appropriate word.

8. *Fully explore readings.*

Sometimes teachers rush through reading tasks without fully engaging students in them. This may be because readings are often too difficult, and once students have tediously figured out all the new words, everyone is tired of the reading. For the development of reading skill, a text should normally not have more than 5 percent new vocabulary. When readings are at the appropriate level, many activities can be used to help students develop in diverse ways. Consider the following possibilities:

Pre-reading

1. Students engage in a discussion to activate prior learning and experiences, preparing them to draw connections between the reading and their own experiences and ideas.
2. Students guess what they will discover in the reading.
3. Students read the title and then write one thing that they hope to learn through the reading.

Reading

1. Students look for specific information as they are reading.
2. Students look for specific grammatical forms or vocabulary as they are reading.
3. Students underline phrases or ideas that stand out to them as they are reading.
4. Students jot down questions they have as they read.

Post-reading

1. Students answer comprehension questions in pairs or groups.
2. Students present questions about the reading to the whole class.
3. Students write and share what they agreed with or disagreed with.
4. Students retell the story or idea in their own words.
5. Students write what might happen next.
6. Students write or share how the reading might apply to their own lives.

Example: A teacher has an adult class read an article comparing different diets around the world. Prior to introducing the article, the teacher asks students to write down what they eat in one day. Students share this information in class and work in small groups to find similarities in their diets. They then guess how diets in other parts of the world may be different from theirs. As students read, the teacher asks them to underline all the food words they see and classify them on a chart she has given. Following the reading, the teacher asks students to work in small groups to answer comprehension questions and also to prepare to share something they learned and something they still do not understand. As homework, the teacher asks students to write down how they might improve their own diet or that of their family.

9. *Use journals.*

There are many ways to utilize journals in language teaching. A class journal can provide a place for students to make public comments, individual journals can go back and forth between teacher and student, or individual journals can be private records of learning which are summarized at the end of the semester for the teacher to read. Student development happens in multiple ways through journaling: by increasing self-awareness, encouraging reflection, and providing a way for teacher and students to build relationships.

Example: A teacher begins a semester by giving each of her university students a blank notebook to use as a journal. She wants them to write specifically about their learning successes and challenges, and their feelings. She instructs them to write in their journals throughout the week and submit them to her on Fridays. She reads through them on the weekend, writes responses, and returns them on Mondays. Several of the students discuss important life issues in their journals, and she enjoys the discussions she is able to have with them.

10. *Use performance assessment.*

How students are evaluated or "graded" is often a tricky issue. In some contexts teachers have no choice but to give a state- or institution-mandated traditional test. However, when feasible, a better approach is performance assessment. This means that the student is evaluated on how well he or she can actually use the English that has been learned. Such performance assessment usually occurs throughout a course, not at the end of it. A type of performance assessment utilizing a task checklist is shown in Appendix A. Performance assessments can include written responses to readings, oral interviews and dialogues, and formal performances such as debates and presentations. Performance assessment is much more likely to promote real language acquisition than are tests that involve memorization of isolated words and grammatical structures.

Example: The goals of an intermediate course include the learning of verb–preposition combinations such as "account for" and "agree with." A traditional approach might be to have students fill in the prepositions following each verb on a test. A more performance-oriented approach might be to have students work in small groups to create and present a short play utilizing twenty of the word combinations they have learned.

Hopefully this discussion on developmental teaching methods, highlighting just a few of the many activities that can help students grow and learn in the English classroom, has brought home the importance of appropriate professional preparation to teach English, as was discussed in Chapter 4. Education in TESOL equips teachers with strategies and skills for guiding learning in the classroom; learning that includes but is not limited to the English language.

MATERIALS

Usually the first question I hear from missionary English teachers is, "Do you have any suggestions for good materials?" The prominence of this question over fundamentally more important ones such as "What kind of training do I need?" possibly stems from our tendency to put the cart before the horse, entering into English-teaching ministries without sufficient preparation or planning. In reality, the training of the teacher and the kinds of methods used are much more significant in student learning than are the materials chosen.

Before we get into a discussion on materials it should be well understood that effective language lessons often do *not* involve paper-based materials. Students may be playing a game, singing a song, engaging in discussion, responding to teacher commands, manipulating real items such as fruits or clothing, and learning English quite effectively without any textbooks or worksheets. It is especially important to be able to use such techniques in resource-poor areas where there may not even be a chalkboard to use, let alone textbooks.

Nevertheless, the question of materials is an important and frequent one. In this section I will first discuss issues surrounding the use of both secular and Christian texts. Then I will discuss other, nontextbook-based approaches to materials in the English classroom.

Using Textbooks

Experienced and trained teachers sometimes view textbooks much less favorably than do novice or untrained teachers. Secular textbook publishing should be seen for what it is: a profit-oriented business. Endless new editions are sometimes prompted more by the desire for more sales than by an actual need for improvements. English-learning textbooks are largely provided by American and British publishers, and as such often have the best interests of those companies at heart, not the students in developing countries who can ill-afford expensive and ever-changing textbooks.

Materials for teaching English are being developed by Christian authors (see Appendix E for a list of resources). Some of these are overtly Christian in nature, and others simply nurture ideas related to faith and/or values. More such materials are needed. But even when considering Christian or "non secular" texts, there are important questions to address. In this section I will outline what I see as cautions in using secular texts, Christian texts, and all texts.

Cautions in using secular texts

1. Some texts portray secular Western values that go against the values of many faiths and cultures. For example, an internationally popular textbook contains a picture of a woman in short shorts and a tank top, which is not public attire in many places.
2. Suggested activities are sometimes not culturally appropriate. One textbook suggests abortion as a debate topic. In many cultures abortion is not a debatable issue, especially not in a public place, and this would not be suitable classroom content.
3. Topics and content may often not suit the local context. For instance, a textbook chapter portraying an American kitchen with a refrigerator, stove, and microwave may have little relevance for students whose homes have a sole kitchen appliance which is a gas wok. The effect of using such a textbook with these students may be that they begin to look down on their own culture, believing that success in life means having an American kitchen.

Cautions in using Christian texts

1. Transparency is of utmost importance, as has been mentioned in several of the earlier chapters. If the text is fundamentally Christian or Bible-based in nature, students should be made aware of this fact before they enroll in the course.

2. The Bible itself is often not an appropriate English-learning textbook. I have seen some very stilted materials that attempt to teach grammatical structures using Bible verses as sample sentences. There are two dangers in this approach. First, sentences which best illustrate the grammar point (and therefore which best meet the students' needs) may not be chosen, because they can't be found in the Bible. And second, this approach can trivialize the purpose of the Bible, which is to teach us about God, not grammar. It is sometimes very appropriate to use a Bible story or a paraphrase as a reading text. However, the Bible should never be used as a source when its level is not appropriate for the students or when its use is distorted, as in focusing on grammatical structures that may be better presented and learned with a different text.
3. Guard against valuing the text more than the students. You may be very excited about having a text that you feel will help your students understand the saving grace of Jesus Christ. However, remember that students may be more likely to see Christ through you than through any Christian materials you choose to use. Be willing to change or adapt Christian materials just as you would secular materials to truly meet the English-learning needs of your students.

Cautions in using all texts

1. Ensure that the text is at the students' correct language-learning level: the i+1 level mentioned earlier. I have visited high school English classrooms where the textbook in use was three or four levels too high. Students had "gone through the book" year after year, without real learning taking place. By high school, the level of the text was badly out of sync with the level of the students. Little real language acquisition can take place when this is the case. If you are teaching in an institution where the text is set and there is little understanding or concern on the part of leadership that the text is too difficult for the students, you can probably still adapt parts of the text and bring in some of your own material which is at the correct level.
2. There is never a perfect fit between what your students need to know and what is in the textbook. Therefore, it is usually appropriate to adapt your text by adding, skipping, or modifying to fit your curriculum and to meet the students' needs and interests.

3. Resist allowing the textbook to become the central focus of the classroom. The classroom should be about students learning and practicing English, which often may not happen best while going through the pages of a textbook.
4. Students in many countries have little money to invest in texts, and whenever possible this investment should be made in textbooks with long-term value, such as grammar resource books, rather than temporary consumable workbooks that cannot be resold.
5. Consider which English skills really require a textbook. Good, leveled readings are time-consuming and difficult to create. Therefore, a reading book or a general English-learning book with many readings might be very helpful. Likewise, a grammar book is often a good investment. Of lesser value are writing texts, especially if you are paying for blank lines on which to write. Writing can be taught well without a text simply by having students write, correct, and rewrite on topics of interest to them.

In listing these cautions I do not want to leave the impression that textbooks cannot foster effective language learning or that they are not a good option. There are indeed often strong reasons for adopting a text. If teachers are nonnative English speakers and do not feel fully confident in their English ability, a textbook may provide assurance for them and their students that the English they are learning is correct. Sometimes an unprepared teacher (either native or nonnative English speaking) may be thrown into a situation where there is little prep time, and the textbook can at least ensure that there is something to study in the classroom. And of course sometimes there is a very good text for a certain context, and the text truly enhances student learning. All of these are good reasons for using course texts.

At this point you may be wondering what the alternative is. If a course text is not used, what are the other options?

Taking a Nontextbook Approach

It is indeed possible to learn a language without going through a textbook. Did you learn your first language using a textbook? No. Do children pick up a foreign language when they move overseas by using a textbook? Usually not. Have you ever known anyone who watched a lot of English movies, listened to a lot of English songs, talked with a lot of English foreigners, and just seemed to learn English without a course or textbook? Probably. So, it is possible to learn a language without a textbook. And one could even argue that language learning which more closely approximates the situations described above is more likely to result in real, usable language skills.

If this is the case, why do so many people believe that a textbook is necessary? One answer to this question is that language learning is often seen as an academic endeavor, rather than as the development of a skill such as learning to play the piano or learning to play volleyball. We see academic learning, such as learning history, for instance, as requiring a text, whereas few people would purchase a textbook to learn how to play volleyball. It is understood that you learn to play volleyball by playing volleyball. Using a language effectively is also a skill that is learned by doing. Classroom learning which does not involve real language use is not likely to promote fluency.

We will see here two approaches to materials that do not involve the use of textbooks and which have as their goal real language use in the classroom: the use of authentic materials and the use of student-created materials.

Authentic materials

A frequent topic in TESOL circles today is *authenticity*. We speak of authentic tasks, authentic assessment, authentic language, and *authentic materials*. These are materials that are not created for English-language learners, but which are found in the real world. Examples of authentic materials include menus, travel brochures, food labels, health advice on the internet, and movie reviews. When students use authentic materials to learn English, rather than materials in a textbook, they are often more motivated and more involved in their own learning. One feels like an actual language user when deciphering a real menu. One feels like a student when looking at a menu in a textbook.

Another attraction in using authentic materials is the flexibility that this approach provides in meeting students' needs. Students need not be using all the same materials, as they usually must when a textbook is involved. Rather, the teacher can meet diverse interests and levels through the provision of different materials. Authentic materials also tend to use more authentic language. Though it is not always helpful to expose learners to how English speakers *really* talk and write, at some point the switch does need to be made from typical learner language to real language use.

There are certainly drawbacks to using authentic materials, a key one being the time required to find and prepare them. Imagine all the pictures in a beginning English text and the time it would take to find all these pictures on the internet, or as real objects, and bring them to class every day. Another difficulty is finding authentic readings at appropriate language levels, or adapting readings for various levels. These can be very time-consuming endeavors. The flip side to this, however, is that usually once gathered, materials can be used for a long time.

In my experience, one of the strongest reasons for using authentic materials is to make the learning more personal. When teaching beginning students words for rooms and furniture, for example, I took digital pictures of my own home, printed them off, and used these for teaching. I followed this with my own written description of my house, at their level. Students then brought in pictures of their own homes, and wrote their own descriptions similar to mine. When teaching family words, instead of using a fictitious family tree in a textbook, I provided students with the names of my own family members and a blank family tree. They then asked questions to discover where certain people fit on my family tree. (This lesson plan is provided in Appendix C.) In these two examples, textbooks are not needed and would have actually diminished the relationship building that occurred through using more personal information.

Student-created materials

Another way to approach the need for materials in the classroom is to view the students themselves as creators of resources. Students can write stories, illustrate, take pictures, and create booklets. Student writing often provides excellent reading material for other students after the teacher has helped the student to edit and correct it. It will often be written at an appropriate level, with a context that is familiar to the other students.

A common approach to textbook organization is to begin with a dialogue. If a textbook is not used, how can the topic be introduced? How will students learn the words and phrases that would appear in a traditional dialogue? Students can often generate dialogues, rather than having information presented to them. Imagine the following lesson sequence:

1. The teacher separates a portion of the whiteboard, and writes "Phrases" at the top. (The teacher does this with each new topic, and soon the students understand what goes in this column.) The teacher designates one student as a scribe who will write the new phrases on the board.
2. The teacher introduces the theme of shopping by showing several items to "sell," handing out play money, and producing a large sign that says

"STORE." She situates herself behind a table or desk, with the sign above her and the items on the desk. She wears a tag saying "clerk."

3. The teacher motions for one student to come to her at the store. She encourages the student to select an item. She elicits from him, or possibly the whole class, the phrase "How much is it?" The scribe writes the phrase on the board.
4. The teacher says, "It's $2.99," and the scribe writes this on the board.
5. The student hands the teacher $3.00. The teacher provides a penny in change, and says, "Here is your change." The scribe writes this on the board.
6. After a few other exchanges during which the teacher elicits additional phrases, the students work in pairs to create their own dialogues. They can use the phrases on the board, or create their own, seeking the teacher's help as needed.
7. Each pair performs their dialogue.

There are certainly times when prepared dialogues are useful or necessary. But I have tried to illustrate here the potential in allowing students to take a larger hand in the development of their own learning materials. Using their own photographs in class, reading their classmates' stories, and writing and performing their own dialogues can all make the classroom more learner-focused and motivating.

If a textbook is not used, it is important that students collect the authentic or student-created materials given them in class in a binder or notebook, creating their own textbook. This provides them with resources and helps them see that they are learning and growing as English users. Such a created text can also serve as a portfolio for the purpose of evaluation.

CONCLUSION

There is no one right approach to the selection of materials. Many teachers may find that a combination of purchased, authentic, and created materials works well. There is also no single methodology that is always appropriate, and there is no one right way to go about creating a good curriculum. What I hope I have shown in this chapter is that what we do in the classroom needs to begin not with the question, "What textbook will I use?" but with, "What are the goals in this learning context?" I hope the point has been made that good teaching uses many different approaches to both methodology and materials. The better a teacher knows his students and the teaching context, the more able he is to make decisions that will reach both language-learning and ministry goals.

DISCUSSION AND APPLICATION

1. Why do you think goals are called the "heart of classroom choices?"
2. Consider a specific English-ministry context. Write broad, specific, and ministry goals for this context, similar to numbers 1–3 on the list of tips for planning curricula.
3. What does the statement that we are in a "postmethods era" mean to you? How might this reality impact English ministry?
4. Choose one of the ten developmental teaching methods discussed. Considering a real English-teaching context, create your own example of this teaching method.
5. Consider a specific English-ministry context. Which of the textbook cautions might be relevant in this context, and why?
6. Develop an idea for a lesson plan that does not use a textbook, but which uses authentic materials, student-created materials, or both. Describe your lesson idea in a short paragraph.
7. Prepare a curriculum for a course in a specific ministry context. Decide what kinds of student materials will be used and what methodologies will be used. Prepare a two- to three-page course guide that could be used as a basis for designing the actual course.

CHAPTER 7

PUTTING IT ALL TOGETHER: MAKING DECISIONS ABOUT ENGLISH MINISTRY

We have journeyed through discussions on potential harms, types of English ministry, and requirements for those seeking to minister through English. We then looked more specifically at models for English-teaching endeavors and at classroom and planning concerns. Now, in this final chapter, I hope to pull together all of this information by providing steps for decision-making about English ministries.

English ministry is likely to originate either with a ministry opportunity or with an individual who feels called to serve in this way. I will outline here two plans of action, one for each of these starting points.

BEGINNING WITH A MINISTRY OPPORTUNITY

In a great many contexts, opportunities to teach English are abundant. Often missionaries face repeated requests for tutoring, conversing in English, teaching English classes in churches, and teaching in schools and universities. Even where English teaching is not requested, doors are often swung open to volunteers. This was my experience when I offered to teach English in the Muslim elementary school in Asia. They had never had a foreign teacher before, but they welcomed my involvement.

The fact that there are few places on earth where English ministry cannot be done has gotten us into trouble in the past. Just because something can be done does not mean it ought to be. I provide here a series of questions and considerations when beginning with a ministry opportunity. Each is based on the information in one of the preceding chapters. I hope this list will help both individuals and sending organizations think through the issues involved before deciding to engage in an English ministry.

1. Chapter 1: Remember that speaking English does not mean you can teach it. Are you certain that you are not considering English ministry on the basis of this widely held misconception?
2. Chapter 2: Consider the potential harms. Is it possible that English learning in your context is contributing to societal, cultural, or educational harm? If you determine that it may be, then the next question is this: Can you help to correct this harm by getting involved? For example, if local languages are being lost, can you help students to value their local language through the content and methods of your English class? Or if local English teachers are losing jobs, can your organization hire local English teachers by starting an English program? If you are not committed to trying to diminish the harms through your English ministry, then I would suggest it might be better not to be involved in teaching English in that context.

   Consider the spiritual harms outlined in Chapter 2. Do you understand what transparency in your setting would entail, and are you prepared to be transparent? Are you committed to ensuring that anyone involved in the English ministry has the training needed to portray the gospel gently and appropriately, and to avoid coercion?
3. Chapter 3: Consider which type of ministry you envision:
   - Ambassador evangelism
   - Host evangelism
   - Ambassador discipleship
   - Host discipleship

   Do you fully understand what is required for effectiveness in your chosen type of ministry?
4. Chapter 4: Consider the personnel needs for this type of ministry. Do you have individuals who are fully prepared with professional, relational, and ministry skills? If you do not have those individuals now, are you committed to finding appropriate personnel or providing training for those who are interested in this ministry? Are you willing to delay initiating the ministry until you have suitable personnel? Are you taking care to consider local national English teachers as potential personnel? Can you ensure that the personnel involved will have sufficient time for preparation and ministry so that both the English-learning goals and the ministry goals will be achieved?
5. Chapter 5: Consider the English-teaching format. Do you wish to develop a program, a course, tutoring, or an event? Are you familiar with the tips pro-

vided for the format you have chosen? Do you have enough and appropriate personnel for this type of English teaching? If needed, have you considered where to find students and how to market this opportunity? Have you considered logistics such as location, scheduling, and start-up costs?

6. Chapter 6: Consider the curriculum, methodology, and material needs. Are you willing to invest in the ministry by purchasing resources for using games, songs, and other developmental activities in class? Will the personnel involved have time and opportunity to choose a good text, or the resources to develop materials?

BEGINNING WITH A PERSONAL CALLING

If you are or would like to be an English teacher who ministers for Christ on the mission field, then ***welcome***! We need more people like you. The steps and questions below are designed to help you think through the process of becoming involved in English ministries.

1. Chapter 1: Remember that speaking English does not mean you can teach it. Are you pursuing training in TESOL appropriate to the type of English ministry that you hope to be involved in?
2. Chapter 2: Consider the potential societal, cultural, and educational harms. Make sure you see the worldwide spread of English for both its pros and cons. Are you equipping yourself with the knowledge and understanding needed to counter some of the harms? If you become the English teacher in an elementary school, for instance, you may be in a position to help other teachers see that the local language is in danger. You may be able to use bilingual activities that would help develop both the native language and English, and your use of such activities may raise the value of the local language and culture in the eyes of others.

   Consider the spiritual harms outlined in Chapter 2. Do you fully understand that as a teacher you will be in a position of authority and that in some cultures students may not feel that they can disagree with you? This may mean that you should not actively seek to lead your students to make decisions for Christ, but should commit to letting them see Christ through your demeanor over the long haul. Are you willing to acknowledge the natural human tendency towards cultural superiority, asking God to make you a humble, learning servant in the environment in which He places you?

Without such attitudes, we contribute to the harms caused by the spread of English, instead of helping to diminish them.

3. Chapter 3: Consider which type or types of ministry you envision:
   - Ambassador evangelism
   - Host evangelism
   - Ambassador discipleship
   - Host discipleship

   If you are a trained English teacher and your entire ministry is teaching English, you may become involved in more than one and possibly all of these. I have simultaneously taught English in an indigenous school (ambassador evangelism), taught English in our own school program (host evangelism), trained Christian teachers in other schools (ambassador discipleship), and taught English in our own seminary (host discipleship). Well-trained English teachers are relatively few in ministry contexts, and you will quickly find yourself having to pick and choose where to spend your time.
4. Chapter 4: Consider your training needs. Aim to become fully prepared with professional, relational, and ministry skills. Resist urgent pleas from mission superiors to arrive on the field before you are prepared, even though the need is so great. The need will still be great later when you are more prepared. If you are just now embarking on TESOL training, consider enrolling in a program at a Christian university. Often such programs combine ministry and English-teaching preparation, helping you to develop the very specific skill set that you will need. If you are a native speaker, make sure that your preparatory program includes the learning of grammar. (Nonnative speakers usually learn English grammar well as they learn English.) You will not have much credibility as an English teacher in many parts of the word if you have no idea what a phrasal verb is or how to explain the difference between simple present and present continuous verb tenses.

   When you arrive on the field, begin learning the local language. Try to reach at least an intermediate level, even if all your teaching is in English. You will be amazed at how much more effective you will be in meeting the specific needs of your students with a foundational understanding of the local language and culture.

   Be prepared to learn from local English teachers. In some places their training may rival or surpass yours. In others they may be poorly trained, but they still can help you understand local perspectives on learning English.

I learned a great deal from my fellow Brazilian and Indonesian English teachers about how certain grammatical structures were taught and learned locally and why certain words and structures were problematic for students in those countries.

5. Chapter 5: Consider the English-teaching formats. As a trained English teacher, you may well be involved in programs, courses, tutoring, and events. You may not only teach, but also be expected to organize and develop these types of English-teaching endeavors. As you have opportunity, gain some experience in each of these areas. Collect information on various types of programs and various course structures. Find out what English-learning structures are prominent in your context and seek to understand them well.
6. Chapter 6: Wherever you serve it is likely that you will be considered an expert on curriculum, methodology, and materials for teaching English. Curriculum is sometimes not addressed at length in TESOL preparation programs. Do some extra study if needed so that you will be able to design courses and programs. Learn as many methods, techniques, and activities as possible, applicable to many different age levels at every language level. If you already know where you would like to work, consider methods, and materials in light of that context. In the Indonesian elementary school where I taught, for example, I had to learn how to create and use portable mini-posters, as I couldn't leave anything in the classroom. Invest in purchasing resources for games, songs, and other developmental activities. These are often applicable to many different teaching contexts and last a long time. Develop a good resource library, and acquire all the materials you can digitally, which is a lot more portable.

CONCLUSION

Why engage in English ministry? Because lives are changed. After all is said and done, if English ministry gives us opportunities to shine the light of Christ through word or deed, then it is worth the effort. I close with statements made by English students who had Christian teachers. These voices would be multiplied by thousands if we could gather testimonials from the many students around the globe whose lives have been positively impacted by Christian English teachers.

In the Words of English Students

"Since my dad is not a Christian, [it is] here at this Christian English school [that] I'm learning how to be a Christian man, by watching teacher Jason."

A teenager

"I know who Jesus is, but I want to know *your* Jesus!"

A university student

"Thank you for your prayer for my baby. She completely healed on Saturday morning, just a day after you and my classmates pray for her. Thank you for your love, kindness and heart for my baby. God bless you."

A mother

"The way you reacted [to a problem in class] taught me how to touch our students' heart. You really change this difficult condition into a very great moment. Thanks."

A teacher

"Thank you for reading this and listen my worry, thank you for praying, thank you for tutoring me not only in grammar, but in my faith."

An entrepreneur

"Let your light shine before men, that they may see your good deeds and praise your Father in heaven."

Matthew 5:16

FINAL PROJECTS

1. Envision an English-ministry opportunity in a specific context. Using the questions asked in this chapter as a guide, write a paper outlining what effective English ministry might look like in the context you have chosen.
2. You have chosen English ministry as your vocation. Using the questions asked in this chapter as a guide, write a personal reflection paper outlining how you will ensure that your ministry as an English teacher is an effective one.
3. Choose a specific context and a specific type of English ministry that you would like to develop in that context. Write a development paper that could serve as a guide for starting the ministry. Include information on goals, personnel, training, curriculum, methodology, and materials. Be sure that your paper shows how this ministry will be effective in both language learning and ministry.

APPENDIX A
English for Life CURRICULUM

WHAT IS *English for Life*?

English for Life is a five-level curriculum for adult and teen learners of English as a foreign language (EFL). It is based on task checklists called Ability Checklists and also includes projects. It does not utilize a textbook. More information and the curriculum guidelines for this system are available by contacting me at jan.dormer@gmail.com. Here I provide an introduction and the task checklists. These checklists may be freely used. Any one of the levels may serve as a curriculum guide for a course. All five levels together may serve as a basis for a full English program.

INTRODUCTION

Central to the idea of *English for Life* is the notion that the best teacher of language is a person, not a book. The idea for this approach was born through dissatisfaction with the perspective that many learners seem to have that going through the book is the goal of a language class. The *English for Life* system stresses class content that is:

- **Communicative:** Use language for *real communication* through reading, writing, speaking, and listening.
- **Contextualized:** Use language for *local* purposes. Talk about *learners' lives.*
- **Edifying:** Use language to stimulate positive *growth* in learners and teachers.

CONTEXTUALIZATION

With many English-learning materials, to change the material is to break copyright laws. Not so with *English for Life*! This system is available digitally, so that teachers can change and adapt it for their own contexts. Currently, these materials are prepared for the Indonesian context. What language is learned and how it is learned, in *your* context, should be determined by student realities and needs. Teachers should use what is given here as a starting point, and further adapt it to meet their students' needs.

CHRISTIAN PERSPECTIVE

This material is an attempt to achieve excellence in language teaching, while encouraging the use of Christian content where appropriate. It has been used in situations where learners are not Christians but are open to developing friendships with Christian teachers and learning about Christian beliefs. It has also been used with Christian students, as a springboard for discipleship and leadership development. With this material, teachers can pick and choose the elements and materials that will be appropriate for a particular group of students, and for individual students.

Some examples of Christian elements are:

- A program of Bible memory. Each checklist tells what scripture is learned at that level. If this is not appropriate for a given context, it can be removed.
- Inclusion of Christians in job descriptions (for example, a banker who is a Christian).
- Inclusion of both Christian and secular curriculum options. For example, in Level 5 teachers can choose to use a "personality test" or a "spiritual gifts inventory."
- Learning to say a prayer of blessing when learning about mealtimes.

THEMES

The thematic content for each level is as follows:

Level	Focus	Content
Level 1	**Basic Vocabulary and Phrases**	Greetings, food, home, family, numbers and money, community
Level 2	**Home and Family**	Introductions, descriptions, jobs, home life, house, schedules, and habits
Level 3	**Community**	The neighborhood, stores, services, directions, professions
Level 4	**The World**	Culture, customs, holidays, geography, countries
Level 5	**Personal Development**	Spiritual life, traditions, beliefs, worldview, spiritual truth, missions

COMPLETION GOALS

After completing all five levels of *English for Life,* a student should be able to:

- Talk easily and fluently about family, self, city and country, and express personal opinions. The student may have errors, but will be able to communicate effectively.
- Understand personal information shared by others and ask pertinent questions.
- Ask for clarification when necessary, demonstrate when he or she does not understand, and continue communication until comprehension is achieved.
- Give and understand social information, such as directions, time, spelling of words, descriptions, costs, quality, etc.
- Read and gain a *general* understanding about worldwide information, such as news articles, information on the internet, or letters received from friends.
- Accomplish basic writing tasks, such as writing friendly letters or writing recipes, though writing will likely have some grammatical errors.

OVERVIEW

Each of the five levels includes eight topical units (Level 1 has ten). Grammar is not addressed specifically in this curriculum but rather will be learned as a by-product of the topical tasks. If more grammar instruction is desired, a basic grammar book can be used alongside this curriculum, beginning in Level 2. I prefer to focus on vocabulary acquisition with incidental grammar learning in Level 1. It is suggested that each unit cover two weeks' instruction, or eight hours of classroom time. Curriculum guidelines for each level are available separately by email. These provide some activities and resources for each topical unit at each level. However, it is important that the teacher who uses this curriculum understand that it is meant to be contextualized by using materials brought in and/or created by both teacher and students.

RECYCLING

An important feature of this curriculum is that content is recycled and revisited at different levels, in different ways. For example, on the topic of food:

- Level 1: Students learn names of foods.
- Level 2: Students revisit names of foods, talk about food preferences and diet, and learn to read simple recipes.
- Level 3: Students talk about food again as they learn to order a meal at a restaurant.
- Level 4: Students compare diets and nutrition in various countries.

Students who have opportunities to review, remember, and build on previous learning in such ways are usually more successful in long-term language acquisition.

PROJECTS

It is hoped that students and teachers engaged in the *English for Life* system will find that their time in class is spent not only learning English, but also engaging in meaningful, interesting, and relevant activities. To promote this concept, a semester-long class project for each level (after Level 1) is suggested. The project activities are inherent in the units, making it possible for students to finish the level having created something that is useful. The projects suggested at each level are:

- Level 2: Home and Family: A booklet for foreigners about Indonesian families and their homes.
- Level 3: Community: A booklet for foreigners providing tips for living in Indonesia.

- Level 4: The World: A video presentation of different areas of the world.
- Level 5: Personal Development: Individual portfolios of personal growth and expectations.

Many other projects are possible. Local contexts and student interests should determine what can be accomplished of lasting value in a semester.

A GENERAL UNDERSTANDING OF TASKS

The list of tasks for each level is provided in the Ability Checklist. Students receive this checklist at the beginning of the semester, and teachers plan their lessons using suggested activities and materials in the curriculum guidelines, or developing their own activities and materials. Class activities should be designed with the purpose of enabling students to check off the "I can" statements on their checklist. An example of teaching activities to accompany this curriculum follows:

Task examples from Level 3:

- ❑ I can give directions to important places in my city.
- ❑ I can understand directions and write them down.
- Provide a map of the school campus. In pairs, have students practice giving instructions to each other on how to find their English class when they come on campus. Practice: turn right/left; go straight/up/down; first door on the right, etc.
- Have students work in groups to prepare written instructions to get from the school to some well-known places in town. Have students compile these written instructions to create a document that would be helpful for a foreigner in this city.
- Have students work in pairs, taking turns giving and writing down how to get from the school to their homes.

INTEGRATION OF SKILL AREAS

This system promotes the integration of reading, writing, speaking, and listening wherever possible. The wording of student tasks sometimes promotes two skill areas, as in the task above, "I can understand (listening) directions and write (writing) them down." But skill integration can also be accomplished by developing class activities which accomplish several tasks. Ideas for this type of integration are provided in the curriculum guides. Teachers will no doubt expand on these ideas, finding additional ways to integrate the four skill areas. For instance, on the subject of Indonesian holidays, various tasks encourage students in effect to "Read, write, and speak about an Indonesian holiday." The sequence below illustrates one way to integrate these skills in classroom activities:

Students will:

- Write a paragraph about a holiday; teacher provides input for student correction
- Exchange paragraphs and read; write three follow-up questions
- Answer questions orally
- Tell a friend about the holiday

ASSESSMENT

This system promotes learner autonomy and relies on self-assessment as the primary means of evaluation. Students decide at what point they feel comfortable checking off items on the Ability Checklists stating that they indeed *can* do those tasks in English. In many places self-assessment is new for learners, and so this system works best accompanied by periodic one-on-one progress meetings with the teacher. These meetings can include student evaluation of their effort in the class and their view of their progress in each of the language-skill areas. This system may not be the most ideal if formal tests and grades must be given.

Ability Checklist Level 1: Basic Words and Phrases

Name: ______________________________ Dates: ______________________

1. **Greetings and Phrases**
   - ❑ I know these greetings: hello, good morning, good afternoon, good evening.
   - ❑ I know these words: please, thank you, you're welcome.
   - ❑ I know this dialogue:

     A: Hi, how are you?

     B: I'm fine, how are you?

     A: I'm fine.
   - ❑ I know this dialogue:

     A: My name is __________. What's your name?

     B: My name is __________.

     A: Nice to meet you.
   - ❑ I know how to say goodbye.
   - ❑ I know these phrases: I don't speak English yet. I don't understand. Please repeat.
2. **Letters and Numbers**
   - ❑ I can say the letters of the alphabet.
   - ❑ I can spell my full name.
   - ❑ I can say and understand phone numbers.
   - ❑ I can count to 100.
   - ❑ I can look at a number up to 100,000 and say it.
   - ❑ I can understand and say amounts of money.
   - ❑ I can ask the question "How much is it?" and provide the correct amount.
3. **Basic Words**
   - ❑ I know these words and phrases: yes, no, more-or-less, not yet, maybe.
   - ❑ I know these colors: yellow, orange, pink, red, green, blue, purple, black, brown, grey, white.
   - ❑ I can describe a color as *light* or *dark*.
   - ❑ I know these words: big, little, good, bad, happy, sad, tired, busy, hungry, thirsty, clean, dirty, late.

- ❑ I know these words: this, that, these, those.
- ❑ I know the basic pronouns and the verb *to be.*

  Ex: I am, you are, he/she/it is, we are, you are, they are.
- ❑ I know these words: where, when, how, why, who, how much/how many.

4. **People**
   - ❑ I know these words: man, woman, child, children, boy, girl.
   - ❑ I know these family words: mother, father, sister, brother, son, daughter, husband, wife.
   - ❑ I know these profession words: teacher, student, pastor, doctor (and words suggested by student).
5. **Days and Months**
   - ❑ I can say the days of the week and the months of the year.
   - ❑ I can use these words: today, tomorrow, yesterday, day after tomorrow, day before yesterday.
   - ❑ I can understand and answer the question, "What day is it today?"
   - ❑ I can ask and answer the question, "When is your birthday?"
   - ❑ I can say and understand years (1985, 2006, etc.)
6. **Food**
   - ❑ I can name ten or more common vegetables.
   - ❑ I can name ten or more common fruits.
   - ❑ I know these words for drinks: water, milk, soft drinks, juice, tea, coffee.
   - ❑ I know these words for ingredients: flour, sugar, oil, butter, salt, pepper.
   - ❑ I know these words: meat, chicken, beef, pork, fish, eggs, rice, cake, cookies, bread, pasta.
   - ❑ I know the words for meal times: breakfast, lunch, supper/dinner, snack.
7. **Clothes and Weather**
   - ❑ I know these words: shirt, T-shirt, pants, shorts, skirt, dress, underwear, socks, swimsuit, jacket.
   - ❑ I know these words: hat, shoes, sandals, umbrella, sunglasses, belt, watch, ring, necklace.
   - ❑ I can describe what I am wearing or what someone else is wearing.
   - ❑ I know these words: sun, rain, wind, hot, cold, wet, dry.
   - ❑ I can describe the weather today.
   - ❑ I can relate the weather to what I am wearing.

8. **Activities and Times**
   - ❑ I know these words: soccer, tennis, swimming, volleyball, basketball, running, walking.
   - ❑ I know these words: reading, sewing, watching TV, listening to music, playing guitar/piano, writing letters, cooking.
   - ❑ I can say the time.
   - ❑ I can say what time I do various activities.
   - ❑ I can understand what time someone else does various activities.
9. **House**
   - ❑ I know these words: living room, dining room, bedroom, bathroom, kitchen, laundry room.
   - ❑ I know these words: floor, wall, window, door, ceiling, fan, light.
   - ❑ I know these living room and dining room words: sofa, chair, TV, desk, computer, table.
   - ❑ I know these bedroom words: bed, closet, dresser, desk, sheets, blanket, pillow.
   - ❑ I know these kitchen words: sink, refrigerator, stove, microwave, counter, cabinets.
   - ❑ I know these kitchen words: plate, fork, knife, spoon, bowl, cup, glass, napkin.
   - ❑ I know these bathroom words: toilet, shower, mirror, towel, soap, toothbrush/paste, shampoo.
10. **Body**
   - ❑ I know these words: face, eyes, ears, nose, mouth, teeth, hair, head.
   - ❑ I know these words: arm, hand, fingers, leg, foot, toes, chest, stomach, heart.
   - ❑ I can say when something hurts.
     Ex: I have a headache. My stomach hurts.
   - ❑ I can understand when someone tells what is wrong with them.

11. **Verbs to Learn throughout the Course:**
    - ❑ I know these words: sit, stand, walk, run, open, close, do, take, give, pray, go, come.
    - ❑ I know these words: read, write, work, study, try, remember, speak, listen, understand.
    - ❑ I can understand commands or requests using simple verbs.
    - ❑ I can make simple sentences about my activities or ideas.
      Ex: I'm reading. I don't understand.
    - ❑ I know these words: clean, wash, cook, iron, fix, use, prepare, tidy/straighten, make, buy.
    - ❑ I know how to make a request.
      Ex: Please cook the meat. Please buy some vegetables.

Ability Checklist Level 2: Home and Family

Name: ______________________ Dates: ____________________

1. **My Family and Me**
   - ❑ I can fill out a form, giving personal data.
   - ❑ I can understand personal questions and respond with information.
   - ❑ I can ask questions about someone else, and understand the answers.
   - ❑ I can tell about my family (physical description, age, personality, hobbies).
   - ❑ I can ask about someone else's family and understand answers.
   - ❑ I can write a paragraph about a family activity (mealtime, shopping, etc.)
   - ❑ I can read a classmate's paragraph about a family activity.
   - ❑ **Vocabulary:** I can label the people on a family tree (nephew, aunt, etc.).
2. **A Family Event (vacation, move, birth, wedding, illness, funeral, etc.)**
   - ❑ I can show pictures of a family event and explain their meaning.
   - ❑ I can look at a classmate's pictures and ask questions.
   - ❑ I can tell about a family event and answer questions.
   - ❑ I can understand an event described by someone else and ask questions.
   - ❑ I can write a paragraph about a past event.
   - ❑ I can read about someone else's event and write follow-up questions.
   - ❑ **Vocabulary:** I know important words for the family events listed above.
3. **Daily and Weekly Routines**
   - ❑ I can write my daily or weekly schedule.
   - ❑ I can read someone's schedule and ask follow-up questions.
   - ❑ I can describe my schedule and answer questions.
   - ❑ I can tell what I am doing at different times of the day and week.
   - ❑ I can ask what others are doing at different times of the day and week.
   - ❑ I can read a description of a daily routine and write a schedule.
   - ❑ I can write a paragraph describing a particular time in my week.
   - ❑ **Vocabulary:** I know words to describe typical daily and weekly activities.

4. **Weather and Clothing**
   - ❑ I can read a paragraph about weather.
   - ❑ I can read a weather map and ask and answer questions with a partner.
   - ❑ I can describe what people are wearing and pictures of clothing.
   - ❑ I can talk about appropriate clothing for different weather.
   - ❑ I can write about changes in weather or dress.
   - ❑ I can read about changes in weather or dress and write questions.
   - ❑ **Vocabulary:** I know words to describe weather, temperatures, and clothing.
5. **Leisure Activities**
   - ❑ I can describe pictures of leisure activities.
   - ❑ I can tell which activities I have or have not done.
   - ❑ I can ask which activities someone else has or has not done.
   - ❑ I can talk about activities that I will do on the weekend.
   - ❑ I can discuss various sports, giving my opinion.
   - ❑ I can write a paragraph describing a leisure activity that I enjoy.
   - ❑ I can read a description of a leisure activity and write follow-up questions.
   - ❑ **Vocabulary:** I know words for leisure activities and sports.
6. **Food**
   - ❑ I can list my typical daily diet and compare my diet with someone else's.
   - ❑ I can understand products and prices in an American grocery flyer.
   - ❑ I can talk about my food preferences and ask questions about someone else's.
   - ❑ I can talk about the food preferences of my family.
   - ❑ I can compliment someone on their cooking.
   - ❑ I can read a simple recipe.
   - ❑ I can read about a food and answer questions.
   - ❑ **Vocabulary:** I know at least 30 food names.

7. **House and Home**
   - ❑ I can describe my home, including rooms, colors, and special features.
   - ❑ I can answer simple questions about my home.
   - ❑ I can ask questions about someone's home and understand their answers.
   - ❑ I can describe my home in a letter.
   - ❑ I can understand and answer questions about my home in a letter.
   - ❑ I can identify common household items.
   - ❑ **Vocabulary:** I know words for parts of the house, appliances, and household items.
8. **Friends**
   - ❑ I can describe a friend, including looks, personality, and activities.
   - ❑ I can answer questions about my friend.
   - ❑ I can make a polite request.
   - ❑ I can extend an invitation.
   - ❑ I can interrupt politely.
   - ❑ I can make an apology.
   - ❑ I can initiate a friendly conversation.
   - ❑ **Vocabulary:** I know important phrases for the above functions.
9. **Christian Content**
   - ❑ I can say the Lord's Prayer.
   - ❑ I can say Psalm 23.
   - ❑ I can list benefits of daily family devotions.

ABILITY CHECKLIST LEVEL 3: COMMUNITY

Name: ______________________________ Dates: ______________________

1. **People in the community**
   - ❑ I can describe people who do different jobs (both character and job descriptions).
   - ❑ I can understand and answer questions about different occupations.
   - ❑ I can read about different professions and answer questions.
   - ❑ I can ask questions about someone's job and explain my job by answering questions.
   - ❑ I can write a description of my job or my ideal job.
   - ❑ **Vocabulary:** I know words for many different kinds of occupations.
2. **Living in a community**
   - ❑ I can describe my community or neighborhood in conversation.
   - ❑ I can ask questions about someone's community or neighborhood.
   - ❑ I can take a phone message.
   - ❑ I can communicate in public places such as the post office or a bank.
   - ❑ I can read about common courtesies needed in a community.
   - ❑ **Vocabulary:** I know words for different kinds of stores and transportation.
3. **Maps, Location, Directions**
   - ❑ I can understand city signs and describe them in English.
   - ❑ I can give directions to important places in my city.
   - ❑ I can understand directions and write them down.
   - ❑ I can ask for help in finding a place when I'm lost; I can give help to a stranger.
   - ❑ I can ask for clarification when I didn't understand the first time.
   - ❑ **Vocabulary:** I know phrases for giving directions.
4. **Health**
   - ❑ I can describe physical symptoms and ask for advice.
   - ❑ I can understand descriptions of physical symptoms and give advice.
   - ❑ I can discuss medicines and how to take them.
   - ❑ I can read about different kinds of exercise and write about my habits.

- ❑ I can read an article about health, take notes, and discuss it.
- ❑ I can share a prayer request and pray about a physical problem.
- ❑ **Vocabulary:** I know words for health care places, medicines, and conditions.

5. **Safety**
   - ❑ I can report an emergency to 911.
   - ❑ I can ask questions about an emergency, such as address, condition, etc.
   - ❑ I can read about safety for foreigners in Indonesia and tell a foreigner how to be safe here.
   - ❑ I can write about a personal experience involving an emergency or safety.
   - ❑ I can read about someone's experience and ask questions.
   - ❑ **Vocabulary:** I know words for emergencies and crimes.
6. **Restaurants**
   - ❑ I can read a restaurant menu and ask questions about it.
   - ❑ In a restaurant, I can: order, ask and answer questions, and ask for the bill.
   - ❑ I can express and understand food preferences.
   - ❑ I can recommend a local restaurant that foreigners might enjoy, in speaking and in writing.
   - ❑ I can pray before a meal.
   - ❑ **Vocabulary:** I know words and phrases for ordering in a restaurant.
7. **Shopping**
   - ❑ I can talk with someone about where and how to buy food.
   - ❑ I can read product labels and ask questions about products.
   - ❑ I can talk with sales people in different kinds of stores.
   - ❑ I can understand a price given in US currency and give the right amount.
   - ❑ I can participate in a typical conversation about paying by credit.
   - ❑ I can write a paragraph related to shopping.
   - ❑ I can read someone's paragraph and write follow-up questions.
   - ❑ **Vocabulary:** I know types of stores and products and vocabulary about payment.

8. **Responsibilities in a Community**
   - ❑ I can discuss civic responsibilities and tell about my involvement.
   - ❑ I can understand and fill out an internet volunteer registration form.
   - ❑ I can read a story about volunteering and take notes.
   - ❑ I can read about a volunteer opportunity.
   - ❑ I can write a letter applying for a volunteer position and answer questions in an interview.
   - ❑ I can compare volunteering in the US and Indonesia in a discussion.
   - ❑ I can give a report about a local volunteer project and answer questions.
   - ❑ **Vocabulary:** I know words related to civic duties and volunteering.
9. **Christian Content**
   - ❑ I can say John 3:16.
   - ❑ I can say 1 Corinthians 13:4–8a, 13.
   - ❑ I can say Galatians 5:22, 23a.
   - ❑ I can say Psalm 121.
   - ❑ I can write about changes and growth in my spiritual life.

Ability Checklist Level 4: The World

Name: ______________________ Dates: ______________________

1. **International Friendships**
   - ❑ I can introduce myself (past, family, job, etc.) to a foreigner.
   - ❑ I can understand a native speaker's description of him or herself.
   - ❑ I can write a one-page letter introducing myself to a foreigner.
   - ❑ I can read a letter from a native speaker, introducing him or herself.
   - ❑ I can read about cross-cultural relationships and share my opinions.
   - ❑ **Vocabulary:** I know 20 adjectives used to describe relationships.
2. **Geography**
   - ❑ I can read about a famous place in the world and answer questions.
   - ❑ I can describe a foreign place which I have visited or read about.
   - ❑ I can answer questions about the place that I describe.
   - ❑ I can watch a video about a famous place, write questions, then discuss my questions.
   - ❑ I can write about the geography of Indonesia.
   - ❑ I can answer a foreigner's questions about the geography of Indonesia.
   - ❑ **Vocabulary:** I know 30 country names.
   - ❑ **Vocabulary:** I know words to describe land, water, elevation, etc.
3. **Lifestyles**
   - ❑ I can explain and answer a foreigner's questions about life in Indonesia.
   - ❑ I can read about life in another country and share with my classmates.
   - ❑ I can listen to a description of a different lifestyle and ask questions.
   - ❑ I can compare different lifestyles and talk about positives and negatives.
   - ❑ I can write about a desired lifestyle change for myself or someone else.
   - ❑ **Vocabulary:** I know names of people and adjectives for the 30 country names that I have already learned (e.g., Sweden, Swede, Swedish).

4. **Food**
   - ❑ I can describe Indonesian shopping, food preparation, and eating habits.
   - ❑ I can write an Indonesian recipe in English.
   - ❑ I can understand explanations of foreign food habits and ask questions.
   - ❑ I can compare Indonesian food with food from other countries.
   - ❑ I can explain my food preferences.
   - ❑ I can read about nutrition around the world and discuss issues.
   - ❑ I can pray before a meal.
   - ❑ **Vocabulary:** I know words describing food, food categories, and meals.
5. **Travel**
   - ❑ I can describe an Indonesian tourist attraction and give advice to foreigners.
   - ❑ I can understand the description of an international tourist attraction.
   - ❑ I can write a letter giving advice to a foreigner coming to Indonesia.
   - ❑ I can answer the questions of a foreigner in Indonesia.
   - ❑ I can find tourist information on the internet; I can understand costs, dates, etc.
   - ❑ I can read tourist information in English and write a letter for information.
   - ❑ I can pray for someone who is traveling.
   - ❑ **Vocabulary:** I know how to talk about Indonesian tourist attractions in English.
6. **Understanding Culture**
   - ❑ I can understand a talk about cultural differences and ask questions.
   - ❑ I can research about a foreign culture and take notes.
   - ❑ I can give a talk about a foreign culture and answer questions.
   - ❑ I can understand a talk about nonverbal communication; I can discuss potential misunderstandings.
   - ❑ I can role play situations in a foreign culture, using appropriate actions and language.
   - ❑ I can write a paragraph on what I have learned about culture.
   - ❑ **Vocabulary:** I know at least 10 words that are used in discussing culture.

7. **Holidays, Festivals, Religions**
   - ❑ I can write a paragraph about an Indonesian holiday, for a foreigner.
   - ❑ I can read about a foreign holiday and write a summary.
   - ❑ I can ask questions of a foreigner about special holidays.
   - ❑ I can answer basic questions about North American holidays.
   - ❑ I can participate in a holiday or tradition from another culture, knowing how to act and what to say.
   - ❑ I can understand a talk about major world religions and write a summary.
   - ❑ **Vocabulary:** I know 20 words for holidays, festivals, and religions.
8. **Reaching out to Others/Missions**
   - ❑ I can read about a world need and answer questions.
   - ❑ I can research a world need and share with my classmates.
   - ❑ I can interview someone about needs abroad and give a report.
   - ❑ I can read two advertisements for charitable organizations and write a comparison.
   - ❑ I can report on an Indonesian initiative in meeting world needs.
   - ❑ I can discuss Indonesia's responsibilities in the world and write a letter recommending involvement.
   - ❑ **Vocabulary:** I know words to describe world needs and problems.
9. **Christian Content**
   - ❑ I can say Psalm 100.
   - ❑ I can say Matthew 5:3–12 (The Beatitudes).
   - ❑ I can read a familiar scripture passage in an easy translation.
   - ❑ I can write (and use!) a list of worldwide prayer requests.

ABILITY CHECKLIST LEVEL 5: PERSONAL DEVELOPMENT

Name: ______________________________ Dates: ____________________

1. **Personality/Spiritual Gifts**
   - ❑ I can take a personality test or spiritual gifts inventory.
   - ❑ I can talk about my abilities and talents in relation to jobs and activities.
   - ❑ I can describe my personality to a friend and answer questions.
   - ❑ I can write a one-page summary of my personality, abilities, and talents.
   - ❑ I can read about someone's personality and ask follow-up questions.
   - ❑ **Vocabulary:** I know 30 character quality adjectives.
2. **Life Story/Testimony**
   - ❑ I can write my personal testimony, suitable for publishing.
   - ❑ I can give my personal testimony.
   - ❑ I can read a short (1–2 pages) biography or testimony and answer questions.
   - ❑ I can ask questions and find out about a person's past.
   - ❑ I can answer someone's questions, telling about my past.
   - ❑ **Vocabulary:** I know the words of life stages.
3. **Life Adventures/Mission Trips**
   - ❑ I can read about an adventure and answer questions.
   - ❑ I can interview someone about an adventure.
   - ❑ I can write a summary of an interview.
   - ❑ I can plan a missions (or adventure) trip, doing research and taking notes.
   - ❑ I can present a talk on a missions (or adventure) trip, using visuals.
   - ❑ **Vocabulary:** I know nouns and adjectives for countries and people.
4. **Change**
   - ❑ I can read about a changed life and understand the main idea.
   - ❑ I can tell about someone who had a significant life change.
   - ❑ I can discuss change and understand why change is difficult.
   - ❑ I can do research about a habit that many people want to change.
   - ❑ I can give a talk about how to achieve a desired change.
   - ❑ **Vocabulary:** I know expressions for habits.
   - ❑ **Vocabulary:** I can describe life change in writing and speaking.

5. **Problems and solutions**
   - ❑ I can read about a problem and discuss it, giving suggestions.
   - ❑ I can write a response to a problem, giving advice.
   - ❑ I can write about a problem, asking for advice.
   - ❑ I can apply biblical principles to a current problem.
   - ❑ I can pray about a problem.
   - ❑ **Vocabulary:** I know words for problems related to marriage, family, and health.
6. **Social/Christian Responsibility**
   - ❑ I can read about a need in another part of the world and answer questions.
   - ❑ I can understand advertising (print and video) requesting charitable donations.
   - ❑ I can do research about a missions project or charitable organization.
   - ❑ I can present a report on the above and answer questions.
   - ❑ I can interview a missionary or volunteer about his or her work.
   - ❑ I can write a summary of my interview for a newsletter.
   - ❑ **Vocabulary:** I know words for natural disasters and social problems.
7. **Ethical Dilemmas**
   - ❑ I can read about ethical issues and discuss my opinion.
   - ❑ I can participate in a group decision on an ethical problem.
   - ❑ I can read about an ethical problem in our society and write a response.
   - ❑ I can write and share a personal point of view on an ethical question.
   - ❑ **Vocabulary:** I know the words and expressions for controversial issues.
8. **Future Plans**
   - ❑ I can understand a talk about goal-setting.
   - ❑ I can list my short- and long-term goals.
   - ❑ I can share my goals and understand someone else's goals.
   - ❑ I can speak clearly about possibilities, probabilities, and certainties.
   - ❑ I can write a final essay about my goals and dreams and read it to others.
   - ❑ **Vocabulary:** I know words and expressions to talk about the future.

9. **Christian content**
   - ❑ I can say the Ten Commandments.
   - ❑ I can say Psalm 1.
   - ❑ I can say Ephesians 6:11–13.

APPENDIX B

A TOPICAL COURSE SYLLABUS

Following is a course syllabus for a class of adult high-beginners. It follows the *English for Life* Level 2 curriculum. Note that this is a planning syllabus, for the teacher's use. A version given to the students would have additional information such as the instructor's name and contact information. It would also probably not have the ministry goals listed as I have here.

Course: Level 2 English: Home and Family

Class times: M/W, 2:00–4:00; 16 weeks

English-learning goal: The students will be able to listen, talk, read, and write about their homes and families using simple sentences and appropriate descriptive words.

Ministry goals:

1. Relational: Relationships will be formed between students and with the teacher through personal sharing.
2. Content: Family, friends, and homes will be seen as gifts from God.
3. Methodology: Students will discover, collaborate, and create, developing skill in application, synthesis, and evaluation.

Course requirements

1. Purchase a course binder and bring it to each class. Organize your course materials in your binder and use them for review at home.
2. Come to each class. The class sessions are your main opportunity to hear and use English.
3. Participate in all of the activities, in and out of class. In this course you will not just be reading a book and doing exercises. You will be working in groups to create things and learn.

Course sequence

WEEKS	TOPIC	CONTENT	CLASS PROJECTS
1–2	**My family and me**	Sharing personal information Physical descriptions Family activities	
3–4	**A family event**	Describing an event Vocabulary for special events Past tense	*Create a booklet describing Indonesian family events (weddings, births, funerals) with pictures and text.*
5–6	**Daily and weekly routines**	Daily activities Times Present continuous tense	
7–8	**Weather and clothing**	Words/expressions for weather and temperature Words for clothing Reading weather maps	
9–10	**Leisure activities**	Words describing hobbies and pastimes Verbs describing activities Future tense Giving an opinion	*Create a slideshow of various Indonesian arts, crafts, and hobbies. Orally explain each slide as you present it to a friend or family member.*
11–12	**Food**	Food words Words for nutritional categories Explaining preferences Verbs and other terms used in cooking Giving instructions	
13–14	**House and home**	Words describing a house Words describing household items	*Create a booklet called "Our Homes" with pictures and text showing each student's house.*
15–16	**Friends**	Words describing personalities Requesting, inviting, interrupting, and apologizing in friendly conversations Initiating conversations	

Assessment

There is no final test for this course. Your grade will be based on your effort and performance in class and will be calculated as follows:

1. Attendance and participation: 30%
2. Bringing the binder to each class and keeping it organized: 20%
3. Completed ability checklists: 30%
4. Contribution to class projects: 20%

APPENDIX C

A SAMPLE LESSON PLAN: FAMILY WORDS

Lesson content: Extended family words, questions, possessives

Time: 60 minutes

Age/Level: Adults/High Beginners

Overall Objectives:

- Students will be able to use nuclear and extended family words.
- Students will be able to ask questions and use possessives in phrases such as "Who is Jason's father?" and "Is Kirsten your sister?"

REVIEW

Time: 10 minutes

Group: Whole class, pairs

Activities

- Show a family photograph. Review nuclear family words (father, sister, wife, etc.)
- Ask one student ("John"), "Who is your mother?" After the student gives the name, ask the class, "Who is John's mother?" Write the sentence on the board. Have them practice in pairs, asking each other the question about John's mother. Emphasize the possessive "s."
- Suppose the mother's name is "Maria." Go around asking students "Is Maria your mother?" Write this model sentence on the board.

Materials/Resources

- Family photograph

Objectives

- Students will remember:
    - Nuclear family words
    - Questions with "who"
    - Yes/no questions with "is"
    - Possessive "s"

LESSON

Time: 25 minutes

Group: Whole class, individuals or pairs

Activities

- Draw a family tree of stick figures on the board, with three generations. Point to two stick figures and ask students to give the two relationship words. Begin with grandma–grandson, and then move to more complex relationships. Write the words on the board.
- Hand out to each student or pair of students (could also be done in small groups if the class is large):
    - Your family tree template with empty squares
    - The names of your family members on small squares to fit the template
- Show students where your name goes on the template. This provides a starting point for questions.
- Students ask questions to find out where the names go. You can point to the model questions on the board, to get them started in asking questions like "Is Jason your son?" and "Who is Joe's wife?"

Materials/Resources

- Family tree template
- Family names

Objectives

- Students will learn extended family words.
- Students will form questions about family.
- Students will use possessives correctly.

Practice

Time: 20 minutes

Group: Pairs, small groups

Activities

- After most students have gotten all the squares in the right boxes, provide the completed family tree, either on a poster or by drawing it quickly on the board.
- Have students play a matching game in pairs. They mix up the names, putting them face down on the desk. Then they take turns picking up two. They need to give the relationship between those two people (e.g., "uncle and nephew" or "daughter-in-law and mother-in-law"). They may look at the poster to remember the relationship.
- "Circle practice": Students pass the names around, one at a time, in a small circle. They ask the student to whom they are handing the name, "Who is this?" and that student must respond with a statement about the teacher's family, such as "This is Jan's brother."

Materials/Resources

- Poster of completed family tree

Objectives

- Students will practice the relationship words
- Students will practice family relationship statements using possessives.

Assessment

Time: Ongoing

Activities

- Listen as students do oral activities.
- Mark names of students on a checklist as either mastering or struggling with question formation, possessives, and/or family words.

Materials/Resources

- Acquisition checklist

Objectives

- The teacher will have an informal record of student mastery.

HOMEWORK

Time: 5 minutes

Activities

- Students will write the names of their family members on small pieces of paper and bring them to the next class. Then students will work in pairs, asking each other questions as they arrange the names into family tree formation on their desks.

Objectives

- Students will have an opportunity to tell about their own families.

APPENDIX D
ORGANIZING AN ENGLISH CAMP

BACKGROUND

I have organized quite a few English camps, in both Brazil and Indonesia. Each has been a major production, bringing teams of foreigners to the field and preparing local teachers and students for leadership positions. After each one I have said, "Never again!" But by the time my fatigue wore off and I could see the many positive outcomes of the camp, I would be ready for the next round.

Here I present details about our English camps in Brazil. I present these ideas not as the right way to do English camps, but as one system that worked well in one particular context. Each location is different, with different goals, resources, and leadership. These ideas may be borrowed and adapted to suit your context.

LOGISTICS

- A five-day residential camp
- English learning through singing, workshops, meal chats, evening skits, evening group work, and social events such as bonfires, square dancing, and sports
- Spiritual emphasis through cabin chats (devotionals), friendship, and some workshops
- 100 campers
- On-site Brazilian leadership team: 20
- Visiting foreigners: 10–20

PURPOSE

Our purpose was primarily to help people know the gospel of Jesus Christ through friendships with Christians. We hoped that participants would enroll in our English school, where we could establish relationships with them as we met their English needs.

LEADERSHIP

BRAZILIAN TEAM

The Brazilian team was largely responsible for logistics: accommodations, game time, meal times, and making sure campers were well cared for. These leaders were prepared through:

- A system of leadership development through gradual progress from camper to leader
- Meetings beginning three months in advance—focus on prayer
- A focus on service—getting things done and meeting people's needs
- A well-prepared series of evening skits and group work

FOREIGN TEAM

The foreign team was largely responsible for conducting workshops on diverse topics of their choosing (crafts, book studies, history, cooking . . . and much more), leading small group teams that we called families, and generally mixing and talking with the campers. These leaders were prepared through:

- Workshops chosen through email dialogue
- Group meetings in the US or Canada prior to coming
- Three days of orientation prior to the camp to plan workshops, learn Portuguese language and culture, and learn how to be a language coach.

All team members were together for two days before the camp to get to know one another, have fun, and pray together. During this time some of the Brazilians taught some of the sessions for the foreigners on language and culture. This was an invaluable time for building team unity.

AN ENGLISH CAMP SCHEDULE

Below I provide the schedule for one of our English camps. Each of our camps had a cultural theme, and this one was Canada. The humorous evening skits featured a Brazilian traveling to Canada for the first time, invariably having a tough time with Canadian realities such as snow and moose and Mounties. Scenic videos of Canada rounded out each evening's presentation.

ENGLISH CAMP SCHEDULE	
Wednesday	
6:30	Supper
7:30	Singing, orientation, introductions
8:15	Division of campers into "Families" (our version of teams)
8:45	Families present name and song or cheer
9:15	VIRTUAL TOUR of CANADA: Eastern Provinces
10:00	Snack
10:30	Cabin Chat (everyone in cabins)
11:00	Get ready for bed
11:30	Lights out
Thursday–Saturday	
7:30	Wake up!
8:00	Exercises
8:20	Breakfast
9:00	Singing
9:30	Workshops
11:00	Break
11:15	Family Competition
12:30	Lunch: Discuss table topics
1:30	Workshops
3:00	Optional Sports
Thursday:	Field Hockey
Friday:	Softball

Saturday:	Flag Football
4:00	Free time: swimming, shuffleboard, ping-pong, showers . . .
4:30–5:00	Water aerobics in English
6:30	Family Supper: sit with your family and discuss talent night
7:30	Singing
8:00	VIRTUAL TOUR
Thursday:	Western Provinces
Friday:	Midwestern Provinces
Saturday:	Ontario
9:00	Evening Event
Thursday:	Square Dancing (basketball court)
Friday:	Wiener Roast (by basketball court)
Saturday:	Talent Show (chapel)
10:00	Snack
Saturday:	AUCTION!
10:30	Cabin Chat (everyone in cabins)
11:00	Get ready for bed
11:30	Lights out
Sunday	
8:00	Wake up
8:30	Breakfast
9:15	Singing
9:30	VIRTUAL TOUR: Territories and Ottawa
10:00	Discussion time in Families
10:30	Group sharing
11:00	Awards and presentations
12:00	Lunch
1:00	Go home!

APPENDIX E

RESOURCES

A few years ago I could have cited all the Christian English-teaching resources that existed in a few short pages. Happily, this is no longer true! Many quality materials have been and are being created by Christian authors, meeting the need for materials that can help us to meet both English and ministry goals. What I have gathered here is just a sampling to get you started. I begin with teacher development resources. Most of these pertain to ministry, as materials for developing English-teaching skills are abundant and easy to find. I then present a list of resources for the English classroom. Again, most of these are Christian in nature, because non-Christian resources are abundant and very easy to locate. Please go to the CELEA website (http://www.celea.net) for a much more complete resource list of Christian materials provided by Kitty Purgason of Biola University.

A Reading List for Christians Preparing to Teach English Overseas

Baurain, B. (2007). Christian witness and respect for persons. *Journal of Language, Identity, and Education,* 6(3), 201–219.

Lingenfelter, J. E. and Lingenfelter, S. G. (2003) *Teaching cross-culturally: An incarnational model for learning and teaching.* Grand Rapids, MI: Baker Academic.

Livermore, D. A. (2006). *Serving with eyes wide open: Doing short-term missions with cultural intelligence.* Grand Rapids, MI: Baker Books.

Pasquale, M. D. (2011). *An ESL ministry handbook: Contexts and principles.* Grand Rapids, MI: Credo House Publishers.

Romanowski, M. H. and McCarthy, T. (2009) *Teaching in a distant classroom: Crossing borders for global transformation.* Downers Grove, IL: Intervarsity Press.

Smith, D. I. and Carvill, B. (2000). *The gift of the stranger: Faith, hospitality and foreign language learning.* Grand Rapids, MI: Eerdmans.

Smith, D. (2009). *Learning from the stranger: Christian faith and cultural diversity.* Grand Rapids, MI: Eerdmans.

Snow, D. (2001). *English teaching as Christian mission: An applied theology.* Scottdale, PA: Herald Press.

Snow, D. (2006). *More than a native speaker: An introduction to teaching English abroad.* Alexandria, VA: Teachers of English to Speakers of Other Languages (TESOL).

Wong, M. S. and Canagarajah, S. (Eds.) (2009), *Christian and critical English Language educators in dialogue: Pedagogical and ethical dilemmas.* New York: Routledge.

BIBLE STUDIES

Bible Studies for New English Speakers by Joan Dungey, R & J Productions.
Twenty-six lesson plans to give teachers lots of hands-on activities to do with students using the Bible as their text.
http://www.eslbible.com

Handbook for Teaching Bible-based ESL by J. Wesley Eby, Beacon Hill Press.
A useful guide for establishing Bible studies with English learners. Bible studies for English learners by Wes Eby include: *The Life of Jesus Christ, What Christians Believe,* and *How Christians Grow.*
http://www.nph.com/nphweb/html/bhol/contributor.jsp?contrib=1710

Passport to the Bible, InterVarsity Press.
This is a study guide designed for international students with advanced English and limited biblical knowledge.
http://www.ivpress.com/cgi-ivpress/book.pl/code=1171

MATERIALS

Adventures in English, Discoveries in English, Exploring English, and *Adventures in Business,* the Evangelical Free Church of America.
Material that is in part Bible-based for multilevel classes where students are at high-beginning to intermediate levels.
http://www.efca.org/reachglobal/reachglobal-ministries/efcaconnect/resources/outreach-english-class

A Window to the World by Doris Edwards, the Jesus Film Project.
English-learning material to accompany the showing of the Jesus Film in the native language and then in English.
http://www.inspirationalfilms.com//wttw/index.html

Common Ground by Michelle Ballou.
A three-level curriculum designed to teach English and character at the same time, especially in international contexts.
http://www.commongrounded.com

English in Action and *English in Action Storyteller* by Wally Cirafesi, the Navigators.
Bible stories taught through Total Physical Response for beginning to intermediate students.
http://www.navpress.com/author/A15184/Wally-Cirafesi

English to Sing and Learn by Jan Edwards Dormer.
Sixteen songs for practicing English, most with Christian topics, along with worksheets for each.
Available free from jan.dormer@gmail.com

Faith Series by Gail Thiessen and Elfrieda Lepp-Kaethler, Providence College and Seminary.
Six volumes of Bible-based student materials: *Faith Journey 1* and *2* for beginners, *Faith Encounters 1* and *2* for intermediate, and *Faith Portraits 1* and *2* for advanced.
http://www.providencecollege.ca/college/bookstore/tesol

New Bridges by Cherie Rempel, Interlink Resources International.
A five-level series for use in conservative cultures (used in Northern Iraq).
Available on the internet to download after purchasing a license.
http://www.go2melik.org/ NewBridgesTextbooks.lsp

Resilience by Michael Medley.

A course for intermediate to advanced adult and young adult English-language learners for building resilience, coping in healthy ways with trauma and stress, and improving English-language skills.

For information about ordering, contact the author at medley@emu.edu.

MATERIALS FOR CHILDREN

God is Good by Jan Dormer and colleagues.

A set of four English workbooks for grades 1–4, for use in EFL contexts.

Contact jan.dormer@gmail.com for more information.

Passport to Adventure, Association of Christian Schools International.

A K–12 English-teaching series being developed for use in EFL Christian schools. As books are published information will be available at the ACSI online store.

http://www.purposefuldesign.com/default.aspx?AffiliateID=1

THEOLOGICAL ENGLISH

Dictionary of Theological Terms in Simplified English: A Resource for English-Language Learners by Debbie Dodd and accompanying Workbook by Cheri Pierson, EMIS.

A valuable resource for English-medium seminaries where students are English learners.

http://www.emisdirect.com/store/books

English for Theology by Gabrielle Kelly Op, the Australasian Theological Forum.

A resource workbook for the development of academic English-language skills in theology for students who are advanced English learners.

http://www.atfpress.com/atfpress/book.php?ID=24

English Language Teaching in Theological Contexts edited by Kitty Purgason, William Carey Library Publishers.

http://www.missionbooks.org

Exploring Theological English by Cheri Pierson, Lonna Dickerson, and Florence Scott, Piquant Editions.

A textbook for English learners, specifically focused on the development of reading skills and vocabulary in the field of theology.

Ordering information can be found at

http://www.exploringtheologicalenglish.com.

Live It! by Jan Dormer.
An intermediate-level English workbook using Christian themes, for seminary students or Christian discipleship.
Available free by email: jan.dormer@gmail.com

USEFUL WEBSITES

Bible Readability: Guidance for choosing the best version for English-language learners.
http://www.eslbible.com/id15.html

Christian English Language Educators Association (CELEA): Download the CELEA News to read about the experiences of other Christian English teachers, find out about conferences, and access Kitty Purgason's list of resources for Christian English teachers.
http://www.celea.net

Speechtree: Provides conversational topics with Bible references.
http://speechtree.caspia.com

Teachers of English to Speakers of Other Languages (TESOL): Access great English-teaching resources, read standards, discover publications, and find out about available courses.
http://www.tesol.org

APPENDIX F

ACRONYMS USED IN ENGLISH TEACHING

ACRONYM	MEANING	USAGE
EFL	English as a Foreign Language	English learning in countries that do not have English as a national or dominant language; English is typically learned as a foreign language subject in school.
ELE	English Learner Education	Emerging in some P–12 school contexts as a designation for the content area; replacing "ESL" in some areas; generally used alongside the term "EL" or "ELL" to refer to learners.
ELL ***EL***	English Language Learner English Learner	Used to refer to students of English, especially in ESL contexts.
ELT	English Language Teaching	Can be used to refer to the field of study, as in "a conference on ELT"; more prominent in EFL contexts.
ENL	English as a New Language	Replacing "ESL" in some places, in recognition that for many students English is not a second, but a third or fourth language.
ESL	English as a Second Language	English learning in countries that have English as a national or dominant language; English is typically learned by children in school or by adults in programs for immigrants.
TEFL	Teaching English as a Foreign Language	Can be used to refer to the field of study, as in "Certificate in TEFL."
TESL	Teaching English as a Second Language	Can be used to refer to the field of study, as in "Certificate in TESL."
TESOL	Teaching English to Speakers of Other Languages	Used to refer to the field of study, as in "master's degree in TESOL."
	Teachers of English to Speakers of Other Languages	An international professional organization of English teachers, based in the United States.
TOEFL	Test of English as a Foreign Language	An English test that is usually taken by foreign students to gain entrance into American universities.

APPENDIX G

PRINCIPLES OF LANGUAGE LEARNING

Principles taken from: Brown, H. D. (2001). *Teaching by principles: An interactive approach to language pedagogy, 2nd Ed.* White Plains, NY: Longman. Explanations written by Jan Edwards Dormer.

COGNITIVE PRINCIPLES

1. **Automaticity**

   Many components of language must be learned to the point of automaticity. When we use a language, we cannot consciously think about all the words and grammar that we are using. Some parts of language must be readily available in our subconscious, to be used automatically.

2. **Meaningful Learning**

   "Meaningful learning will lead to better long-term retention than rote learning" (p. 57). Language learners need to understand the language that they are hearing and using, and the topics discussed should be of interest to them.

3. **Anticipation of Rewards**

   Learners are driven by the anticipation of rewards. These may be "tangible or intangible, long term or short term" (p. 58). Language learners need a reason to learn the language.

4. **Intrinsic Motivation**

   Language learning is most successful when there is intrinsic (internal), rather than extrinsic (external) motivation. When language learning stems from the learner's needs or desires, the learner is said to have intrinsic motivation. A learner who only has extrinsic motivation will often give up during the long haul of learning a language.

5. **Strategic Investment**

   Language-learning time should be invested wisely in activities that result in real language acquisition. Clear learning goals and an understanding of personal learning styles can help the learner to use language-learning time strategically.

AFFECTIVE PRINCIPLES

6. **Language Ego**

   Learning a new language involves developing new ways of "thinking, feeling, and acting—a second identity" (p. 61). This new and different self can cause learners to feel uncertain and defensive at times.

7. **Self-confidence**

   Successful language learners are self-confident language learners. They believe that they can achieve their language-learning goals.

8. **Risk-taking**

   Successful language learners are willing to make mistakes. They are willing to take risks, and therefore they have more opportunities to learn through both successes and failures.

9. **Language-Culture Connection**

   Learning a language also involves learning about cultural values and different ways of thinking. Successful language learners understand that using a new language may involve expressing ideas and feelings in very new and different ways.

LINGUISTIC PRINCIPLES

10. **Native Language Effect**

    A learner's native language can both facilitate and interfere with learning the new language. Words that are similar in both languages ("cognates") will help in language learning, but features that are different may interfere with the language-learning process.

11. **Interlanguage**

    All language learners go through a developmental process during which time they use the language imperfectly. A learner's interlanguage should be seen as progress, not as a failure or a refusal to learn.

12. **Communicative Competence**

    If communicative competence is the final goal, then language-learning activities need to focus on the skills needed for effective communication in authentic contexts. These skills include fluency and accuracy, as well as the ability to use language appropriately in real-world contexts.

REFERENCES

Abelaira, T., Butzbach, G., Ghosn, I. Ong, M. F. and Parsons, A. (2004). Responding to job competition from native English speakers. *EFLIS Newsletter.* November 4(2). Accessed March 12, 2007 from http://www.tesol.org/s_tesol/sec_issue.asp?nid=2994&iid=2996&sid=1

Bahloul, M. (1994). The need for a cross-cultural approach to teaching EFL. *TESOL Journal, 3,* 4–6.

Baurain, B. (2007). Christian witness and respect for persons. *Journal of Language, Identity, and Education, 6*(3), 201–219.

Bloom, B. (1956). *Bloom's Taxonomy.* Downloaded Dec. 27, 2009 from: http://www.officeport.com/edu/blooms.htm

Braine, G. (Ed.) (1999). *Non-native educators in English language teaching.* Mahwah, NJ: Erlbaum.

Brooks, J. G. and Brooks, M.G. (1993). *In Search of Understanding: The Case for Constructivist Classrooms.* Alexandria, VA: Association for Supervision and Curriculum Development.

Brown, H. D. (2001). *Teaching by principles: An interactive approach to language pedagogy, 2nd Ed.* White Plains, NY: Longman.

Byler, M. (2009). Confronting the empire: Language teachers as charitable guests. In M. S. Wong and S. Canagarajah (Eds.), *Christian and critical English Language educators in dialogue: Pedagogical and ethical dilemmas* (pp. 120–130). New York: Routledge.

Chamberlain, M. (2009). First, the log in our own eye: Missionaries and their critics. In M. S. Wong and S. Canagarajah (Eds.), *Christian and critical English Language educators in dialogue: Pedagogical and ethical dilemmas* (pp. 46–52). New York: Routledge.

Cummins, J. (1994). Semilingualism. In *Encyclopedia of language and linguistics,* (2nd ed.). Oxford: Elsevier Science.

Cummins, J. (2000). *Language, power, and pedagogy. Bilingual children in the crossfire.* Clevedon, England: Multilingual Matters.

De Mejia, A. (2002). *Power, prestige and bilingualism: International perspectives on elite bilingual education.* Clevedon, England: Multilingual Matters.

Dormer, J. E. (2006). A perfect blend?: A study of coworker relationships between native English-speaking and nonnative English-speaking teachers in two school sites in Brazil and Indonesia. Unpublished doctoral dissertation, University of Toronto, ON.

Edge, J. (2003). Imperial Troopers and Servants of the Lord. *TESOL Quarterly* 37:4.

Fennes, H. and Hapgood, K. (1997). *Intercultural learning in the classroom: Crossing borders.* London: Council of Europe.

Johnston, B. (2003). *Values in English language teaching.* Mahwah, NJ: Lawrence Erlbaum Associates.

Johnston, B. (2009). Is dialogue possible? Challenges to evangelicals and non-evangelicals in English-language teaching. In M. S. Wong and S. Canagarajah (Eds.), *Christian and critical English language educators in dialogue: Pedagogical and ethical dilemmas* (pp. 35–45). New York: Routledge.

Kachru, B. B. (1985). Standards, codification and sociolinguistic realism: The English language in the outer circle. In R. Quirk and H. Widdowson (Eds.), *English in the world: Teaching and learning the language and literatures* (pp. 11–36). Cambridge: Cambridge University Press.

Kaining, L. (2003). Chinese. In J. Lo Bianco and C. Crozet (Eds.), *Teaching invisible culture: Classroom practice and theory* (pp. 53–100). Melbourne: Language Australia Ltd.

Krashen, S. (1981). *Second language acquisition and second language learning.* Pergamon Downloadable from: http://www.sdkrashen.com/SL_Acquisition_and_Learning/index.html

Kumaravadivelu, B. (2006). *Understanding language teaching: From method to postmethod.* Mahwah, NJ: Lawrence Erlbaum Associates.

Livermore, D. A. (2006). *Serving with eyes wide open: Doing short-term missions with cultural intelligence.* Grand Rapids, MI: Baker Books.

Loptes, K. A. (2009). A preliminary survey of Christian English-language teachers in countries that restrict missionary activity. In M. S. Wong and S. Canagarajah (Eds.), *Christian and critical English language educators in dialogue: Pedagogical and ethical dilemmas* (pp. 53–59). New York: Routledge.

Makoni, S. and Makoni, B. (2009). English and education in Anglophone Africa: Historical and current realities. In M. S. Wong and S. Canagarajah (Eds.), *Christian and critical English language educators in dialogue: Pedagogical and ethical dilemmas* (pp. 106–119). New York: Routledge.

McKay, S. (2002). *Teaching English as an international language: Rethinking goals and approaches.* Oxford: Oxford University Press.

Paul, D. (2003). *Teaching English to children in Asia.* Hong Kong: Longman.

Pennycook, A. (with Sophie Coutand-Marin). (2003). Teaching English as a missionary language (TEML). *Discourse: Studies in the Cultural Politics of Education. 24/3,* 337–353.

Pennycook, A. and Coutand-Marin, S. (2003). Teaching English as a missionary language (TEML). *Discourse: Studies in the Cultural Politics of Education. 24/3,* 337–353.

Phillipson, R. (1992). *Linguistic Imperialism.* Oxford: Oxford University Press.

Phillipson, R. (1999). Voice in global English: Unheard chords in crystal loud and clear. In B. Seidlhofer (Ed.), *Controversies in applied linguistics* (pp. 51–62). Oxford: Oxford University Press.

Priest, R. J. (2008). *Effective engagement in short-term missions: Doing it right!* Pasadena, CA: William Carey Library.

Purgason, K. B. (2009). Classroom guidelines for teachers with convictions. In M. S. Wong and S. Canagarajah (Eds.), *Christian and critical English language educators in dialogue: Pedagogical and ethical dilemmas* (pp. 185–192). New York: Routledge.

Romanowski, M. H. and McCarthy, T. (2009) *Teaching in a distant classroom: Crossing borders for global transformation.* Downers Grove, IL: Intervarsity Press.

Robison, R. (2009). Truth in teaching English. In M. S. Wong and S. Canagarajah (Eds.), *Christian and critical English language educators in dialogue: Pedagogical and ethical dilemmas* (pp. 255–264). New York: Routledge.

Schiller, H. I. (1976). *Communication and Cultural Comination.* White Plains, NY: Sharpe.

Smith, D. (2009). *Learning from the stranger: Christian faith and cultural diversity.* Grand Rapids, MI: Eerdmans.

Smith, D. I. and Carvill, B. (2000). *The gift of the stranger: Faith, hospitality and foreign language learning.* Grand Rapids, MI: Eerdmans.

Snow, D. (2001). *English teaching as Christian mission: An applied theology.* Scottdale, PA: Herald Press.

Snow, D. (2006). *More than a native speaker: An introduction to teaching English abroad.* Alexandria, VA: Teachers of English to Speakers of Other Languages (TESOL).

Snow, D. (2007). *From language learner to language teacher: An introduction to teaching English as a foreign language.* Alexandria, VA: Teachers of English to Speakers of Other Languages (TESOL).

Snow, D. (2009). English teachers, language learning, and the issue of power. In M. S. Wong and S. Canagarajah (Eds.), *Christian and critical English Language educators in dialogue: Pedagogical and ethical dilemmas* (pp. 173–184). New York: Routledge.

Tennant, A. (2002) The ultimate language lesson. *Christianity Today, 46(13).* Downloaded on Dec. 5, 2009 from http://www.christianitytoday.com/ct/2002/december9/1.32.html

TESOL (2003). TESOL position statement on teacher quality in the field of teaching English to speakers of other languages. Downloaded on Dec. 5, 2009 from http://www.tesol.org/s_tesol/bin.asp?CID=32&DID=374&DOC=FILE.PDF

Woodward, M. (1993). Teaching English as a tool of evangelism. *Journal of Applied Missiology, 4(1).*

Wong, M. S. (2009). Deconstructing/reconstructing the missionary English teacher identity. In M. S. Wong and S. Canagarajah (Eds.), *Christian and critical English Language educators in dialogue: Pedagogical and ethical dilemmas* (pp. 91–105). New York: Routledge.

Wong, M. S. and Canagarajah, S. (Eds.) (2009), *Christian and critical English language educators in dialogue: Pedagogical and ethical dilemmas.* New York: Routledge.

INDEX

D

E

F

W